Papa's Shoes

and other stories of life

Edited by
Mark Worthing, Pete Court and Claire Bell

ISBN 978-0-6486957-0-7

Compilation copyright © Mark Worthing, Pete Court and Claire Bell 2019
Copyright of individual chapters remains with the author of those chapters.

All rights reserved. Other than for the purposes and subject to the conditions prescribed under the Copyright Act, no part of this publication may be reproduced, stored in a retrieval system, or transmitted in any form or by any means, electronic, mechanical, photocopying, recording or otherwise, without the prior permission of the publisher.

Cataloguing-in-Publication entry is available from the National Library of Australia http:/catalogue.nla.gov.au/.

This edition first published in 2019

Cover art and typesetting by Morton Benning

Published in Australia by Immortalise via Ingram Spark

www.immortalise.com.au

Sponsors

We wish to thank the following organisations for their sponsorship of the Stories of Life creative writing competition and publishing venture:

 **Tabor College of Higher Education** – sponsor of the 2019 Stories of Life Open Award for stories up to 1500 words.

 **Eternity Matters** – sponsor of the 2019 Stories of Life Short Award for stories up to 500 words.

 **Lutheran Schools Association** – sponsor of the 2019 Stories of Life Youth Award for stories up to 1000 words by writers 17 and under.

Thanks also to **1079 Life** for their help with promotion and support for Stories of Life.

Contents

Introduction 1
Papa's Shoes 2
   Valmai Redhead
Kosciuszko Tough 4
   Hannah Morrison
God Fixed the Scanner 8
   Julie Willersdorf
Sprinkler Spontaneity 11
   Diana Davison
The Happy Memoir 15
   Baxter Gierus-Heintze
The Answer 18
   Anusha Atukorala
Hearing God's Voice 20
   Graham Byrne
That Crazy Message from God 22
   R.J. Rodda
A Cab Trip 24
   Peter Evans
God's Garden Gloves 26
   June Hopkins
My Mother's Death 30
   Jonah Teh Kai Xuan
Drop Zone 31
   Juni Desireé Hoel
One of the Six 33
   Craig Chapman
She Called Me Mouse 36
   Bronwyn Fisher
On My Dirty Knees 40
   Sally Shaw
I Like Boys 44
   Jane Walker

He is Alone	47
Rosalind Lum	
More Than a Piece of Paper	52
Hannah Matthews	
Arise	56
Claire-Louise Watson	
Out of My Depth	59
Teri Kempe	
Son of Man	63
al Bikaadi	
A Sheep Called Jeffrey	68
Margot Ogilvie	
The Answered Prayer	72
Mikaela Tan Shyi Ern	
Heart Wide Open	74
Angela May	
John Jenner	78
Olivia Harman	
Jamie	82
Kaye Johnson	
No Place like Home	86
Gaynor Faulkner	
I Raise a Hallelujah	90
Yasmin Esther	
The Golden Detour	93
Kaitlin Turland	
God My Confidence	96
Ivan Yap	
Three Seconds, Bus Stops and Log Trucks	97
Megan Higginson	
In a Manger	99
Joanne Prenzler Smith	
A Thousand Dollars	101
Rusty A Lang	
Only God Knows	102
Priscilla Ng	

My Journey Climbing Mount Kinabalu 104
    Leanne Low
A Good Friend 107
    Jemuel Wong
A Lesson for Life 109
    Alan Blunt
A Certain Stranger 111
    Kylie Gardiner
An Inclusive Church 113
    John Alexander Duthie
A Stranger Passing Through 116
    Maria Rudolph
The Unlikely Tractor Pull 119
    Lisa Holbrook
Story of My Life 122
    Joyce Ling
Confessions of a Realist 124
    Emily Maurits
One Blue Arrow at a Time 129
    Naomi Currie
The Circle of Love 134
    Liisa Grace-Baun
Vessel 138
    Rebecca Abdel-Nour
Good Out of the Bad 142
    Leanne Chong
Rebirth 144
    Kylie Gardiner
The Dress 148
    Jane Owers

Introduction

This is the fourth year of *Stories of Life* and once again we have been surprised by the variety and depth of extraordinary stories of faith that continue to come in. This year in particular we wish we had room for more stories in the anthology as there were so many quality entries in this year's *Stories of Life* competition. We sought to include here a range of the best stories from this year's entries that represented the diversity of experiences of God's grace in individual lives. Many of the stories in this volume are happy tales of wonderful encounters and blessings. Others are gripping stories of personal heartache. There are stories from school students and stories from people born before the Second World War. There are stories from those born in Australia and those who have migrated to Australia, and a growing number of international contributions. There are stories of near death experiences, the loss of a child or parent, dramatic journeys and finding God in everyday relationships and experiences.

The stories this year were submitted in three categories: Open (1000-1500 words), Short (up to 500 words) and Youth (500-1000 words). A team of judges has awarded prizes to the top three stories in each category, which have been generously donated by sponsors Tabor College of Higher Education, Lutheran Schools Association and Eternity Matters. We are also indebted to 1079 LIFE which promoted the competition and continues to air many of the stories during January and February of each year. We also wish to thank our judges this year: Simon Kennedy, Kit Densley and Ruth Bonetti.

Special thanks also must go to May-Kuan Lim, who has again done much work behind the scenes organising the website, communicating with contributors, organising workshops and many other activities that have made the smooth running of Stories of Life possible.

Finally, we wish to thank all of those who participated in this year's *Stories of Life* competition. It is our hope that the stories selected for this year's anthology will be an encouragement and blessing to all who read them.

Mark Worthing on behalf of the 2019 editorial team

Papa's Shoes

Valmai Redhead

The shoes were exactly where I had put them, hidden away out of sight and out of mind, yet never quite forgotten. I lifted them carefully out of the cupboard and attempted to smooth out the minute creases in the vintage leather. They seemed so tiny, so perfect, and so delicate.

My husband had worn them when he was taking his first steps more than sixty years earlier. These little shoes held feet that ran to play. Those same feet would drag slowly to the school bus and walk with obedience to Sunday school. Later, protected by steel-capped boots, they would stride with excitement towards machinery and climb into the cab of many a big rig. With a flourish of romance they would lead his bride down the aisle, squeezed into less familiar brown dress shoes. Over the passage of time they would relax, wearing his favourite moccasins, as he nestled on the couch with his own children watching cartoons on television or reading a story.

Now his tiny first shoes had a new reason for being. Celebrating the dedication of our baby grandson was their moment to be passed on to the one who carried his name. Even though the two of them had never met, they were a poignant legacy. Somehow their worn stitching edged our family story. My fingers seemed too big and almost clumsy as I grasped them. Their once pristine white had dulled a little with age. I began to straighten the T-straps, fastening them one at a time around the dainty button at each side. With gentleness I wiped a damp cloth across the perforated decorations on the top, then tucked some crumpled tissue paper underneath. The 'Little Toddlers' trademark was still quite visible. A few days later I removed the paper, and with great care I carried them to be mounted and framed. The lady understood exactly what I wanted to do. As we tried different combinations our spirits seemed to dance together in perfect unity. We adjusted the position of the shoes to look natural and not too staid. I handed her the printed verse from Psalms to be placed underneath: 'The steps of a good man are ordered by the Lord.'

Back at home I began to write. Creativity mingled with my tears as the words formed themselves: *'Dear Archie, before your Papa went to heaven he knew your second name would be Laurence, just like his. The name Laurence means joyful, and it certainly was a joyful day when you were born ... God has directed the steps of every generation of our family. May he also guide your steps throughout your life.'*

Before wrapping the precious gift, I attached a copy of the letter at the back. One day, when Archie is older, he will read it and can pass on the story to his children. Wherever his future steps lead, I hope he will always treasure the precious legacy of his Papa's shoes.

Kosciuszko Tough

Hannah Morrison

At 5:20am, the pre-dawn chill pried open my eyes. Three blankets and a sleeping bag were not enough for the subzero Jindabyne night. Swapping my pyjamas for jeans and boots, I pulled on my head-sock. I grabbed my gear and enough food to last all day. And water, lots of water. No one needed that much water, but Mum said we had to—just in case. In case a storm whips up and we're stuck up there for days on end? Unlikely.

After a quick breakfast and a half hour drive through the winding mountain roads, Mum pulled into the deserted carpark. Thredbo Village was as quiet as a stage with no actors. As we strode through the automatic doors, there was only one man in the shop, fishing through a box of jackets. He stepped behind the counter to serve us.

'One family lift pass,' Mum said. 'Return please.'

'Bit windy up there today,' he warned. 'That'll be $68. The last lift leaves the top at 4pm. If you're too late, you can walk down the track under the lift.' With the Kosciuszko Express lift pass sorted, I left the shop, trailed by my little sister and Mum. Excitement hummed in my bones. Months of training, of hiking hills and kilometres of bush; they prepared us for today. Not long into our ride the chairlift began to sway in the breeze. Mum gripped the bar so tight her knuckles paled, and I bit my lip to avoid laughing at her. She never liked heights, but she got really annoyed if I laughed at her when she was scared. The mountains loomed all around us as we rose above Thredbo Village toward the weather station. When the chairlift shuddered, I stopped joking. Would it be too windy to walk the track today? That would be so annoying. I looked down at the trail weaving through the trees. That mountain bike track looked like fun. We lost sight of the path as the lift arrived at the top. Only a few steps toward the walking track and I knew we had a problem. As we walked past the end of the building, gale force winds hit us. We ducked back behind the shelter of the building, plastering ourselves against the wall. Mum pulled out her phone and checked the weather. Wind gust speed was sixty to eighty kilometres an hour!

www.ingramcontent.com/pod-product-compliance
Lightning Source LLC
Chambersburg PA
CBHW052044300426
44117CB00012B/1960

That's craziness, I thought. My little sister gave me a worried glance. At only eight years old, she was smaller than my ten-year-old height of 150cm, but she was strong for her age. She'd be okay. We stood up and edged around the corner. Only a few steps away from the wall Elle started to whine.

'Tuck in behind me,' Mum suggested, and we walked single file. It was easier, but we wouldn't get very far at that speed. Elle slumped to the ground.

'Hold her hands, we'll pull her.' Mum and I held her hands and tugged.

'It's too hard,' she moaned. 'I can't do this.' Every time she stood up the wind pushed her little body backwards until she almost fell. Leaning over like an old man, she gripped Mum's hand.

'C'mon Elle, you can do it. Just a few more steps.' Mum turned to me. 'Make a wall, like a stone wall to stop the wind.' Mum and I stood shoulder to shoulder. Leaning into the wind about a 20- or 30-degree angle, Elle took shelter behind us. All very well for her, but now it was super hard for us! Shoulder pressed to shoulder we plodded on and she walked a bit faster than a turtle, and that's being nice. The metal track we walked on was better than the dirt trail I'd expected. The hike would have been easy without the wind. I hated the wind.

We came to a ladder and stopped for a well-equipped hiker coming down. He looked absolutely trashed, which set off alarm bells in me.

'I've been up there three nights. I haven't slept, just got pummelled by the wind and it wrecked my tent last night. I've had enough. I'm getting out of here,' he mumbled. I had to wonder if we would give up too. If a seasoned hiker bailed, what chance did we have?

'Come on. Keep going. You can do it. Come on...' Mum repeated herself for the next hour.

About half-way up the track, we stopped at a lookout. Elle looked totally spent. I was okay, just a little tired. Mum wore that stubborn don't-mess-with-me face.

'We'll probably have to go back,' she announced, pulling out her drink bottle for a sip.

My face fell. *But we can see the summit! How can you give up now?* I knew better than to voice these thoughts.

'Let's sit for a few minutes. Have some food and see how Elle is, okay?' My attention turned to the food. As we ate, I stewed, huddled behind the boulders at the lookout. Small mountain peaks surrounded us. The metal boardwalk wound through a rocky, treeless valley before disappearing behind a peak in the distance. The snowy tip of Mt Kosciuszko shined white beyond there. My frustration grew.

The plan for today was a 13km walk in around four hours. Get to 2228m above sea level and achieve our goal of the highest point on mainland Australia. They rested, and I waited, pacing around the freezing lookout to stretch out my stiff legs. I checked my watch. 11:05 am. We'd already taken two hours to get here from the lift.

'You've got to give her time,' Mum's gentle voice pleaded with me. I plonked down on the ground again. The wind seemed to ease. My hope grew a little.

'I think I can keep going,' a little voice said. Relief filled me and I bounded to my feet.

'Let's go!' So, we did. Elle still needed a wall to walk behind, and the occasional pull, but we made steady progress toward the summit.

'Come on. Keep going. You can do it.' Those words strengthened us, and we walked on. And on. And on. I kept telling myself that the summit would be worth it, and ten more steps came easily.

'Look! Brumbies!' Elle squealed. Sure enough, two horses raised their heads about 100m away. 'Aren't they beautiful?'

'They're just horses.' I muttered. Mum gave me The Look. I rolled my eyes and walked on.

Though it was summer, a few patches of snow lay on the shady side of the mountain. Near the final stretch, we met a guide who showed us how to ski with our feet, like without skis. Glissading, he called it. I tried to glissade down the snowy slope, but I fell on my face. The guide made it look easy. Elle laughed at me. It wasn't funny.

The last kilometre to the summit was fun—the track spirals around in a circle and a pile of rocks marks the top with the official sign. Elle and I raced up the slope. But when I got to the top, I was unimpressed. Mt Kosciuszko was only slightly higher than the other peaks that surround it. The nearest one, Mount Townsend, at 2209m, wasn't much lower than the summit I stood on. It would be more impressive if God had made Mt Kosciuszko to stand out on its own. The wind still blew fiercely, but I didn't care anymore. After a quick lunch break we headed back down the track.

After we'd seen the summit, my enthusiasm vanished, and so did my energy. I felt dead on my feet. The only problem: the chairlift was still six kilometres away. With the wind at our backs now, Elle strode on at a decent speed. She just kept going and going. It was my turn to whinge.

'Can we have a break? My legs hurt.'

'You'll be okay,' Mum said. 'Let's get to the next bend.' I peered down the track to where she meant. It wasn't too far away. 'You're stronger than you think you are,' she whispered. 'God made your muscles strong.' I'd give anything for a mountain bike to take me back down. But I put one foot forward, then the other. At the bend, we took a quick rest and walked on.

'Come on, let's finish this.'

Six hours after we'd first stepped off the chairlift, we finally returned and rode down to the carpark. To this day, whenever we're struggling, Mum reminds us we're 'Kosciusko tough.' We take the next step forward, and even when it feels too hard, we can keep going. And before we go hiking, we always check the wind conditions.

God Fixed the Scanner

Julie Willersdorf

The phone rings. It's Monday morning. I and seven of my children had gathered in the lounge room for our daily Bible sharing time. The call interrupts our time. It was my husband, Ian, who had left very early that morning for work with son Benjamin traveling to Cooma, over three hours away. We run a livestock contracting business and he was pregnancy scanning sheep.

'The scanner's not working. There's a crack in it. You'll have to get Paul to meet me halfway with the other scanning head.' He sounded flustered.

'How will you both get the work finished?'

'Paul will have to ring the other client and cancel today's work.'

This didn't make sense to me. Paul was about to head off to work also scanning sheep, but in another direction. They had an extra full week of work and had decided the night before to swap jobs as there were more sheep to scan with the Cooma job and Ian was faster at scanning than Paul. Paul wouldn't have been able to finish that job in the one day. Ian would barely finish the job in a day. It would mean finishing later than normal. However, it was the only way to fit in all the work for the week.

With having to meet halfway, they both would lose over three hours out of their day, making it unlikely for Ian to finish his job for the day as well as Paul. No, this didn't make sense, not just to my mind, but I couldn't see how God would allow such pressure to be put on both father and son and jeopardise not only today's work but also the work for the rest of the week.

To trace steps back a couple of years, our business had been struggling, owing the tax office quite a substantial amount of money. At that time Ian and I had been challenged to surrender things to God so we decided to give our business to God. We began to see miracle after miracle as we honoured him in our decisions, surrendering the way we operated things and doing it God's way. However, it got to a stage over one weekend where we looked like losing the business and our house. But God intervened and again showed us the way forward.

Since then, whenever we make wrong decisions without asking the Lord's direction, he gets our attention some way, such as our bank balance dropping drastically. So this decision for Ian and Paul to have to travel so far and both lose so much time, not to mention the cost of the fuel, seemed not how God would run his business. Reluctantly I told Paul to go to the shed and get the other scanner ready to take to Ian. While he was getting it the rest of us, who were still in the lounge room, sat pondering the situation.

One of the children, Rohnen, suggested, 'Why don't we pray?' The evening previous to this we had been watching, 'Faith like Potatoes,' and had been inspired by Angus Buchanan with his simple trust in God. Now was a chance to put it into practice. And often it is the faith of a child which also inspires and which takes the lead. Rohnen continued, 'If God can make the whole world from nothing and can make man, surely he can fix something that man can make.' It sure sounded simple and made sense. Did we have that faith?

This same boy had made a similar statement on another occasion when we could not open our wheat grinder after it became jammed. I had tried and tried but it would not budge. An older son went out the back to the shed to get a tool to help open it. Rohnen made mention of the reading in the Bible we had read earlier that morning, how God does not trust in the strength of men's legs, or something like that. He said that God could open it and why don't we pray. So I asked him to pray. I tried again to turn the grinding part and it turned and opened. Just then my other son returned with tool in hand ready to open it for me but stood and looked amazed, asking who was it that got it undone. We looked at each other and chorused, 'God did!'

So with the remembrance of that time and the inspiration of Angus Buchanan, I said, 'Okay! I'll ring dad back.'

I dialed Ian's number. We waited for him to answer. With the words and simplicity of what Rohnen had said, I felt everyone in the room had an expectant faith. Ian answered with a stressful, 'Yeah, hello,'

'Ian, I don't think it's a good idea for Paul and you to drive all that way and lose so much time.'

'What else can we do? The scanning head has a crack in it.'

'Remember it is God's business. I'm sure he wouldn't want to put you and Paul under so much stress and waste so much time so that the rest of the week is more stressful.'

'So what do you suggest?'

'Well, shouldn't we at least pray? Shouldn't we see what he wants? I'm sure there must be another way. He could fix it if he wanted to.'

'Okay. You pray then.'

'Lord, this is your business, and you know that the scanner is not working. It doesn't seem right having all this stress put on Ian and Paul having to travel so far, losing time and putting pressure on the rest of the week. We know you can do all things so we pray you will fix the scanner.' Everyone said a loud 'Amen!'

Ian called out, 'Benjamin, check the scanner again and see if it is working.'

There was a pregnant pause. Before we heard Benjamin reply, 'It's working!'

Praise the Lord! The crack was still there, but God somehow fixed the scanner!

Sprinkler Spontaneity

Diana Davison

I used to be a 'gym junkie' in my youth. Now I'm older, I have morphed into a 'walkaholic'. Over the years I had clocked up many kilometres walking around the local park in my neighbourhood. I usually relish these moments. A ritual spent breathing in the mornings with a sense of vigour, enjoying the serenity that nature brings, and starting my day on a positive.

But this one day, after months of a creeping decline, was very difficult. I was struggling. Depression's quicksand was beginning to swallow me whole. Each day, life was becoming harder to manage. I was thankful for the routines of my children. They unwittingly kept me going. However, at that point, I was transformed into someone only just pulling it together. From my appearance, I was normal on the outside but on the inside, more fragile than the wings of a butterfly. Look closer and one could see the cracks.

I tried to function as best I could. I didn't know when my 'normal' would return. And so I continued my regular medicine of walking around the park's perimeter, dragging a soul full of grief… the mourning kind.

At the end of my final lap, I took a seat. It wasn't a strenuous walk so stretching seemed pointless. I just simply sat on the park bench, staring blindly. The muted conversations in my head turned into a lingering with the Lord. It was brief. I didn't want to impose. Feeling at a loss in all directions and suffocating with it, I needed help. I was so empty, drowning in my emotions. The deepest grief imaginable became my constant shadow after my father's passing, less than a year ago.

Sitting quietly, I noticed mounds on the oval's grass surface, next to the football goal posts in the park. Were they new? I thought it weird I hadn't noticed them before, given the number of times I had walked this area and thought I knew every inch of it like a memorised classic movie, citing the stand-out lines before they were said… or had I not been paying attention all these months?

The park was deserted, apart from the few who were left to soon escape the day's late morning heat. It was a few minutes after eleven o'clock in the morning. A windy day that failed to blow life into me. I was alone and feeling it. A split second later, after sharing my private one-sided conversation, my attention was suddenly seized. The ground of the park's oval closest to where I was sitting, some twenty feet away, seemed to burst open with wet flare. Three dutiful sprinklers made their presence known, like frolicking whales spouting water in play.

The sun glared down at the scene while I aimlessly sat, depleted. I wondered if this was somehow a sign, a response, a something to my ramblings. I looked on and waited. All three long fountain jets of water were spread out with good intention and distance apart. Each synchronised in changing the direction of cool wetness. I noticed they rotated periodically. The playful wind grabbed the heavy spritz of water vapours, blowing it vigorously around. Each escaping fine mist flew off to thin out like a dying smoke screen. I viewed on, wastefully wishing I could walk underneath each one, to lose myself in the moment. But, such a carefree move was lost to a spirit so empty. I was weighed down by my own thoughts and feeling older then I should.

My quiet pondering was interrupted by two women, each with a dog on a lead, and one little boy of around seven years old. Without pausing, the boy instantly ran beneath the closest sprinkler and tried to dodge its watery aim. His laughter free and joyful with not a care in the world. The larger of the two dogs tried to take a bite at the stem of the water bolt. The smaller dog barked and tried drinking the water. Its small frame first flinched away but became bolder with every lick. Meanwhile, the women held onto their leads and giggled from their safe distance, making sure they didn't get wet. I was lost in observation, my face grinning and damp... from tears. They only stayed a couple of minutes to enjoy this sprinkler splashing sojourn before continuing on their way.

Alone again, I stayed seated for a moment longer. I then got up and walked over to my nearby parked car. Unlocking its door, I sat behind the wheel but continued to look at the spraying sprinklers.

Sprinkler Spontaneity

But then, in a surprising moment of clarity, I was shot with an idea to 'just do it!' Oddly, the thought of 'why not, who's judging?' spurred me on. No one was around. I can frolic under the sprinklers if I want to. My mind came to life. I don't have to be a child to enjoy such innocent treats. The most basic things in life can be the most giving. I will get wet and dance or merely stand under a raining sprinkler if I want to. Who cares if I am soaked? It will dry. I should embrace the opportunities when they present themselves. Have no regrets. The message in my head was loud and clear.

I got out of my car and walked over to the middle sprinkler. I stood and welcomed it with open arms. The water hit me on the face like a water gun to its easy target. It was cold. It felt good and strikingly refreshing. My smile was as pure as the liquid that drenched me. I wanted more. A fleeting thought crossed my mind... 'Why did I even hesitate?'

After three slow laps around the sprinkler, I was drenched and I was feeling so much happier. I had almost forgotten about the simple pleasures in life and its uplifting effect. I finally allowed myself to let go and enjoy every second of this chance act of fun. Reluctantly I stopped. It was time to go. I headed back to my car again and sat watching the sprinklers in silence. This time I was smiling. My teeth were even showing.

Within ten minutes, one by one the sprinklers turned off and moved to another part of the field. Each arm of water extended for as long as possible to stay alive. Each landed spray mimicked the morning dew that had fallen earlier to gradually soak the blades of green carpet. The mounting of drops pooled to form puddles. A nourishing reserve.

As for my soaked clothes, they would soon dry off. With every minute I stayed wet it reminded me of what I had just done. I was feeling lighter and thankful my plea had been heard. This watery cleansing helped me change my frame of mind and reminded me to live in the moment. Life does and will get tough. It is meant to be an undulating journey to experience, not a flat line.

* * *

I went back to the same spot again three days later. This time I took to my walk pounding the pavement with more positivity in my steps and with lungs filled with the air of appreciation. I could hear the birds calling out as if to cheer me on. The wind, too, ushered me forward with the sun radiating down on me. It knew my brightness was my own.

Hot from exercising, and aware of the park's sprinkler timing, I was present and ready. When they came on I walked over to the middle sprinkler without faltering and did my three laps again. Yes, it was truly invigorating.

When I was done, I made my way to my car. Taking a moment to look over my shoulder, I saw a magpie had swiftly swooped in and taken my place. It frolicked with happy hops while enjoying its birdbath. I admired it and thought to myself... I know how that feels, and walked away beaming with gratitude.

The Happy Memoir

Baxter Gierus-Heintze

It was July. I glanced out the window. It was school holidays. My family was in our Ford Territory, heading for who knows where.

The time was very questionable to have a road trip. It was about 4.30 pm, the time where families would start preparing dinner, or heading home from work.

I looked in the front.

My family weren't happy, weren't enjoying themselves like a usual road trip. We had Mum, Dad, Grandma, Auntie Cathy, my sister, and me.

We turned onto Palmer Road.

Suddenly, a feeling of dread overcame me.

99 percent of the time, when my family turned on Palmer Road, I knew where we were going.

Estia Homes. Where dear Gran was. Now don't get me wrong, I love going there. However, the time of the trip, plus the state of my family, made me feel that Gran was not well.

She wasn't.

I hesitated to go in, but I wanted to. It would be okay.

It wasn't. When I stepped into her room, number 57, I gasped in horror.

I'd seen Gran when she wasn't well. But tonight was much worse.

She couldn't speak. She couldn't do anything other than lay on her bed. She looked like she was shrivelled up like a dried prune.

I had my thoughts. Would she understand me? Would I be able to understand her? Would I get sick? I felt really sick inside, like the time when my Grandma went into Intensive Care for blood clots. A quick glance around the room made my stomach churn violently.

At least that wasn't the case here. But I still was very reluctant.

The thoughts, the conscience, roared at me. Should I have this moment? Should I…

'Here. Come here,' Mum called. 'She wants you.'

Phew, I sighed. Luckily, I didn't have to make the decision myself!

I grasped Gran's hand. 'Goodbye Gran,' I whispered. 'Go with Jesus.' Then I turned and walked away.

I thought of the lovely memories that we had together. Friday was good. That was three days ago. There was no bickering between me and my sister. We had a really lovely time with Gran. There were no medical issues, like Gran's legs hurting. I felt God was present. No, I *knew* God was present.

Everything went right that day.

It all went wrong 24 days later.

July was nearing its end. August was just around the corner. Where I could really consolidate my studies, dig deep, and home in on more A's.

Holidays were tough. With dear Gran of course, and Grandma taking regular trips to the hospital, we didn't have time to do much else. We had plenty of late nights due to Grandma. We stayed in Adelaide *long* after dark not once, but twice.

Now was school time. I stood up and read the poem *The Geebung Polo Club* in front of the entire class.

Ring! The phone rang.

'Moshi moshi?' Miss Webb hollered into the phone. (Okay, she didn't *actually* say that) 'Yeah, he's reading a very enlightening poem about two polo teams killing each other... Yes? ... Okay. After this. Ciao.'

'You have to go sign out after this. Make it count!'

I began reading. '*It was somewhere up the country, in a land of rock and scrub...*'

I felt really confident. This poem I rehearsed over and over, and I could almost say it without cue cards. But I had them up there just in case.

When I was done, everyone applauded me (even though they were bored). However, I wasn't stuck up the front trying to dwell on their uninterested, bored, miserable faces. I raced to SSO. I thought we were going to take Grandma home from the hospital.

WRONG.

That day, all was not well.

She looked horrible.

She looked as pale as a white Holden. Unlike Gran. We managed to understand her. Just.

The then unthinkable was now inevitable.

She. Would. Not. Live. …

My certainty came true when Grandma plummeted. Some, along with me, decided to leave. But before that, I read Psalm 100 for her, my favourite psalm, while sobbing uncontrollably.

'<sob> *Shout to the Lord, all the earth…*'

When I had finished, she said thanks. 'God bless,' she muttered.

That was it.

On the way home, I thought. Although the day was downright terrible, there were many miracles. For example, Grandma was in good hands at this hospital. They were all nice staff.

Next, Grandma wasn't in too much discomfort for long periods of time. That was a big miracle.

Finally, she had us. She had her family by her side. Some people don't have their family around them. And she had God. She stood by him and was not afraid in the face of death. She had all her loved ones and God with her. The big miracle is she had faith in God. She still hung on to her faith. Just like Gran. She said she was going to be fine. We didn't think so. She *knew* she was fine – spiritually. Because she had faith. Faith that she would be safe in the arms of Jesus.

Nothing else mattered.

The Answer

Anusha Atukorala

One dreadful day, anxiety snuck in through my back door—an unwelcome intruder who ambushed me when I was least expecting it. Each time I thought the sneaky beast had left, he reminded me of his presence, grabbing me firm in his grasp. *How I longed to be free!*

One morning, I sat at my desk, my Bible open but with tears blurring my vision. I felt alone, sad and fearful. Then ... in the silence, I heard a whisper in my heart.

'*You need a friend.*'

A friend? I reflected for a few moments. *Why of course*! A praying friend who walked this journey with me could make all the difference. I picked up my pen and wrote down the names of five friends I could trust. I circled one. Beautiful loving Sophie (not her real name) had come to mind very often. She lived far away, but distance is never an issue for prayer or between friends.

'Lord, would you send me some encouragement today? I need it so badly.'

I wiped my tears.

'And Papa, if you think Sophie should help me, would you ask HER to write to me?'

When I checked my emails, I found two messages—both were from my list of five. My first prayer had been answered! *Wow*! I wrote back, sharing my heart with my friends and asked them to pray for me. My heaviness lifted.

I logged onto Facebook and saw there was a message awaiting me in my in-box. When I saw who'd written, my heart turned a somersault and a smile began to dance on my lips. I wrote asking my friend if she could help me. Her response when it came, stunned me.

Oh! I think this is definitely of God. Wait until you hear my side of the story. I've been thinking of you a lot the last few days. And then today I was driving to town and while I was still on our property I felt incredibly convicted to pull over and send the message then and there. It was like I knew I couldn't go one metre further, I HAD to do it then.

I am delighted to see God's direction so clearly in this ... of course it's a 'Yes'. I'd love to be that person for you. My circumstances have changed so much. I'm not that busy person anymore. I have deliberately stepped back from so much with the intention of greatly deepening my relationship with Jesus.

So there you go—it sounds like it has His fingerprints on it don't you think? I am so honoured and excited to be your Hand-holder. Let's do this. Let's trample this thing for good!

Much, much love,
Sophie

Tears rained down my cheeks for the second time that day.

But now ... hope sang a sweet melody within.

I knew I would be okay.

Hearing God's Voice
Graham Byrne

Some years ago I was Acting Chairman of the Public Works Standing Committee (PWSC) SA.

The Chairman of that Committee became very sick with Asthma and Emphysema and was admitted to the Royal Adelaide Hospital (RAH) intensive care.

I felt I should visit him and rang the hospital to check if that was okay. I was told only next of kin could see him, but the nurse said, 'Graham while you are on the phone, I will tell him you have called.'

She returned to say 'if it is only you Graham, and not the boys (the other MP's on the Committee) he would like to see you.'

I was somewhat surprised and wondered what to do.

There was an old Bible in a drawer in my office. I simply opened it and read 'the priest will take holy water in an earthen vessel'.

I knew that the Lord was the priest and I would be the earthen vessel taking holy water when I visited him. When I visited him, the next night, I said simply 'hallo!' But then, 'To be honest I have come to pray for you.' I knelt at his bedside and prayed.

I have an amazing letter at home written by his secretary saying how he had been in a sense 'strangely warmed' as a result of my visit.

He came out a few days later quite well.

The exact words of his letter to me are as follows:

'I write to thank you for visiting me at the RAH last week. Your kind words put a great feeling through me and removed many anxieties.

Knowing that I am not a religious person, the relief that I felt was profound. Your prayer assisted me during a very difficult time.'

The sequel to this was that a few years later 1999 and again in 2002 I became very ill myself and underwent heart surgery at Ashford Private Hospital. I growled at a nurse when I saw air bubbles in a tube connected to me. I then felt bad about that and when her senior nurse Mary came, I said how sorry I was at my earlier reaction.

Nurse Mary said to me – 'Don't worry sweetie, we know how you feel, would you like me to pray for you.' She knelt at my bedside and prayed for me.

I felt the Lord say to me then:

'See Graham, what I'll do for you when I ask you to do something for me.'

That Crazy Message from God
R.J. Rodda

'Would you like to borrow my car for a while?' My friend Naomi indicated her battered blue Mazda. I could hardly refuse. Although the public transport in Melbourne served me well enough during the day it was less frequent and more unsafe at night. There was another consideration too. Peter.

We had started a small youth group at our church, leading it together as friends. A tall young man who brimmed with energy and enthusiasm, Peter was also very good-natured. After each youth event, he would ferry me and all the other youth home even though we lived scattered around the eastern suburbs. With a car, I could help.

One night, Peter asked me to drive Alisha home while he took the rest who needed lifts. I agreed, even though I was feeling very tired. Alisha slid into the passenger seat, her heart-shaped freckled face glowing with youthful prettiness. She filled the car with bright conversation. I struggled to keep my eyes open and respond appropriately back.

The dark road stretched before me, empty of cars. I turned to respond to Alisha and saw a red light flash past. I had just driven through a red traffic light and I hadn't even seen it! Cold fear clutched at me but I did not pull over. Instead I pretended to Alisha that nothing was wrong, trying to keep myself awake by gripping the black plastic steering wheel and ignoring the little voice inside my head that suggested I stop driving. Because what would we do then? How would we get home?

A car horn beeped behind me. It was Peter's car. He should have been in another suburb dropping the other youth off instead he indicated that I was to follow him. Bewildered I did so, pulling over at the nearest petrol station.

Once there I fumbled out of the car and leaned against it, the cool night air sharpening my dulled senses. Peter came over to me and said, 'I'll drive you and Alisha home'.

Overwhelmed with gratitude but confused, I stammered out my surprise at his words and his sudden appearance.

'God told me to come and find you and drive you home,' he said.

I was utterly astounded. When God spoke to Pete, it must have sounded completely crazy. How would he find me in the many streets of Melbourne? And yet in obedience he came after me.

So I handed him my keys and he took us home. Looking back I don't even remember how he got back to his car. All I know is that God used Peter to rescue us from my dangerous driving and worse, my stubborn pride that had not admitted I needed help.

A Cab Trip
Peter Evans

Sometimes we would get a call over the two-way from the base to pick up a parcel, or a bag or such. On other occasions we would be told, 'No, not a parcel, a body', meaning a normal passenger. Or, just as helpfully, 'The fare will be waiting in the foyer for ya'. It was all very droll.

To collect one 'body' I had to climb just one level of an old rooms-for-rent building in the inner city, knock on the old gent's door, carry his bag to the boot and head off with them both to Mascot International Airport. Taxi life is hard and tiring and the dollars not easy to come by. This was probably a $20.00 fare (early 1980's) compared with maybe $3.00 or $4.00 for short runs within the CBD, and time was important. Nevertheless, this dear old bloke, visibly not very financial, spoke quietly to me about his 'stick'. We hadn't been driving long but he'd left it behind in the room he'd just vacated. Between pauses and my occasional prompts because I was interested, he talked about its importance to him, how he came by it and so on.

I imagined it was a walking stick - replaceable easily enough - and I just let what he was saying go in one ear and out the other; especially since he didn't seem likely to have the money to pay for the return trip to go back and retrieve it; and every turn of the wheels was taking us closer to our destination.

There was a plane to catch of course, which wouldn't be likely to wait, and besides we were almost there. Yes, he said he didn't have the money to go all the way back. But yes, he was very early for the plane's departure (back to the States, Chicago) and yes, he would be very pleased if I drove him back for free. The stick turned out to be nothing more than a greenish bough torn off a tree branch, about walking stick size. What on earth…? Why did I do that?

On the way back, we got talking about eternal matters, as you do, and he shared a dream that sounded to me more like a vision, an actual supernatural experience. It had happened many years ago, when he was a lot younger, and it didn't make a lot of sense to him. But, like the stick, it was important enough for him to remember and repeat it. It was something significant that happened even though he didn't understand its meaning.

Fortunately, he was in the right cab. I was able to interpret his dream; at least I gave him my understanding of what I thought it might mean. He said, 'You speak such beautiful words'. It transpired that his heart was for God and that God had actually placed a call on his life through the experience that he was explaining to me. However, he didn't have anyone who could explain its meaning or the way of salvation to him.

I did my best and told him God had loved him for a long time and wanted him to be with him forever. He only needed to respond and say, yes. Jesus would forgive everything he had ever done wrong. I said, 'Just tell the Lord you now understand, and you accept his sacrifice on the cross for you. That's what the message was about. He wants to give you eternal life, come into your heart and give you the joy of knowing him.'

This man obviously had a soft heart toward his Maker and didn't need a whole lot of encouragement or additional explanation. He'd been ready for a long time. I let him dwell on the Lord's extraordinary love and grace, to reflect that even though it had taken so long God had nevertheless not forgotten him, and today was his day. I told him we would see each other and the Lord together in heaven.

So, for the second time, the cab took the main turn-off into Mascot International Airport and this time we stopped outside Departures, and I opened the boot. A congenial porter came to help the old chap with his bag. As they started to leave together, I remember handing that excuse for a walking cane to the porter and saying, 'Take care of the stick'.

God's Garden Gloves
June Hopkins

These days, I wield a mean pair of secateurs, but it was not always so. In 2012, widowed for two years and rattling about in a high-set, five bedroom, brick home on my own, I was lonely and restless. My four adult offspring were all happily married, living in their own homes, and busily reproducing. I had lived for forty years in the same house and knew all my neighbours, the butcher, the baker and lots of other people.

The voice of God to my inner self was more than a whisper. *Take a risk. Move.* I knew it would be wise to down-size and move to a smaller, low-set home. There were a lot of 'buts'. But, I will miss everybody I know. But, how will I start again? But, will I be able to find the right place to suit me as I grow older? I knew I needed to trust God to guide and provide and so I put my home on the market. It sold and the purchaser wanted vacant possession in four weeks.

The search to find a suitable new home became urgent. My son drove me around a suburb where I would be close to two of my daughters. The search didn't take long. He pulled up in front of lovely low-set, cream brick house.

'What about this one, Mum?' He smiled encouragingly at me.

I liked the exterior of the house, and I loved the interior, plus the price was right. There was just one catch. Surrounding the house was a spectacular garden. Bright flowering shrubs filled garden beds in front of the house and all around the back.

'I don't know anything about gardening,' I admitted with a wry expression worthy of more than one emoji. My husband had always looked after the garden at our home, although at best it was always minimal and rather nondescript.

A good friend, well known for her gardening expertise, suggested she could mentor me if I bought the property.

'You'll love gardening, once you know what you're doing,' she assured me. I pictured myself looking like she did in her garden, with floppy broad brimmed hat, garden gloves and carrying a trowel or secateurs. Somehow the image didn't seem like me. I rather like sedentary, intellectual pursuits such as writing and jigsaws, but I was sufficiently persuaded by my friend's enthusiasm that I decided to make an offer on the place.

I asked to have a second look inside, to help me make decisions about what furniture would fit and what I needed to sell. The agent arranged the second inspection and I was surprised to find the current owner at home. We looked at one another and realised that we had known each other years before. She was an active Christian.

'You are God's choice for this house, and he has chosen this house for you,' she said with a hint of excitement.

'Really?' I felt amazed by her firm statement.

'A group of women from my church helped me prepare for sale. They washed every wall in the house, and as they did, they prayed for God to bring in the person he wanted to own the house. That person is you, and I know you would have been praying for him to lead you to the right house for you.'

I nodded, feeling humbled and overwhelmed.

God is so good, I thought but I continued to feel somewhat daunted by the lovely garden. I wondered how long it would take before I managed to destroy the plants.

After I moved in, my gardening friend visited. I followed her around the garden with a notepad and pencil. Over two hours, she named each and every plant and gave me care instructions.

'That's a Kalanchoe. Water it when the soil is dry, but don't wet the leaves. Trim off dead bits. It likes sunshine and sandy soil.' Dutifully I wrote down her instructions.

'That's called Crossandra. Keep the soil moist and don't let it dry out.' We progressed from shrub to shrub. I began to imagine myself looking after the plants. I was astonished that each plant had different needs for care. My friend taught me when and how to prune the various plants. She gave me a gift of a shiny new pair of secateurs.

'Secateurs are a gardener's best friend,' she told me, giving me an encouraging pat on the back. She told me the various other garden implements I would need, and the names of fertilisers and weed controlling solutions.

I began to care for the garden, albeit a little diffidently. It was then that I discovered that God wanted me in gardening gloves, wielding secateurs. The house I had purchased occupied a corner block. Across the road from the side fence was a small park and children's playground, and beyond that a local shopping centre. There was a steady stream of foot traffic past my house every day. At any time people walked past on the way to buy a few essentials from the shops. Every afternoon mothers took small children past to play in the park. Mornings and afternoon all sorts of people walked their dogs.

As I worked in my garden in the cool of the afternoon, I got to know so many people. I learned the names of all the dogs – Sunny and Skip, (two little terriers), Bingo, (a Corgi), Brutus, (a gentle Labrador), Oscar and Charlie, (Poodles), Fred, (a Basset Hound named after the cartoon character), and many others, as well as at least three cross breed dogs named Max. I'm not sure why Max is such a well-loved dog name. My own small dog, Rusty, was equally a drawcard for conversations.

I chose to initiate conversations as people passed by while I snipped dead leaves off my plants. I learned people's worries and interests. One lady talked about losing her daughter to cancer and is now rearing a grandchild. Another talked about her grandson being killed when crossing a road when a truck thundered through the intersection. I listen. I share my faith when I feel it is invited, and I pray for these people. One passer-by at a time, I began to make new friends.

A neighbour, who has access to left over bread from a bakery, brings me a variety of unusual loaves I might never otherwise eat – sourdough, rye, multigrain –as well as choice dinner rolls and sliced white bread. Another neighbour brings me bags of lemons and mandarins from their trees.

Each afternoon, as I pull on my gardening gloves, I thank God for them, and for the provision of this house, my garden and my new friends. I have lived here seven years now and know I am exactly where God wants me to be. Praise God for secateurs and garden gloves.

My Mother's Death

Jonah Teh Kai Xuan

My name is Jonah. I don't have a normal family. I am an only child, which means I do not have siblings. My family isn't rich or poor either. My dad was a DJ while my mother was a programmer. I also have a loving grandmother who loves God very much. In this story, I will talk about a tragic event which happened in my life when I was four years old.

About two years after I was born, my mom had leukaemia. It is a blood disease, and she needed some treatment in the hospital. After another two years, I was four years old. I did not expect my mother to die so quickly. It happened on a morning on December, at around 3 a.m. while I was sleeping. When my dad woke up, he saw my mother lying on the couch motionless. God had already taken her to heaven. My dad called an ambulance and that was the last time I ever saw my mother.

My dad was very sad when he saw her die. For him to not feel so heartbroken, he drank a lot of alcohol and became drunk. He hated God for taking away my mother. He stopped going to church. My grandmother and I were also very sad. I cried all night and when my grandmother saw that I was crying, she cried together with me. I did not know God yet, but my grandmother loved God and she shared the gospel to me over the next two years. I finally accepted Christ into my life.

After a while, I stopped crying over my mother's death. I would still feel sad, but I would focus on reading my Bible and started to show how much I loved God. Eventually, my dad also realised that this was all part of God's plan. He started going back to church and started becoming a good Christian. Before I came to my Christian school, my dad would always share some Bible verses to me and pray with me. After I joined a Christian school, I started to learn even more about God. I realised that whenever a bad thing or tragic event happen, we may not understand why it happens. However, what we know is that God still loves us and is always there for us. Since that event, I always remind myself to not hate God when something is taken away from us.

Drop Zone

Juni Desireé Hoel

Gabby held out a plate of freshly backed cupcakes coated with chocolate icing and rainbow sprinkles. Lindsey and I each grabbed one.

'Oh my God, yum!' said Lindsey.
'Oh my God, yes!' I said.
'What?' said Gabby.
'Huh,' we looked at her.
'That's what God is saying.'
'What?' said Lindsey.
'You said his name,' said Gabby.
'Yeah, so,' I said, shrugging my shoulders.
'When someone calls your name, you wait to hear what they have to say to you.'

Lindsey and I stared at her blankly.

'Well, you called God's name and he's waiting,' she said.

Lindsey and I looked at each other with a smirk.

Oh, so Gabby must be a Christian, I thought.

She ran this after-school program called Drop Zone with four others, and I looked up to her because we both had long dark brown straight hair. When you're in Year 7 and don't fit in because you're an unfashionable nerd, our similar hair made me feel connected to her.

She often pulled me up on how I used God's name flippantly by using the 'What?' tactic, and over time, it caused me to start taking God seriously.

I'd believed in God since I was a little, but I never interacted with him or thought he interacted with me. I never even thought about him, but Drop Zone put God on the radar for me.

I went to Drop Zone every week for the two years they ran it and, while not many people went, I loved it. There was a Super Nintendo, arts and crafts, games, and food. But most of all I loved that these five people welcomed me. They had this knack of bringing up God in everyday conversations and they showed me he was relatable and that it wasn't weird to talk about God or to God.

Ten years later I ran into Gabby at my local church where I was now a youth leader hanging out with teenagers each week with games and food. We both still had the same long dark brown straight hair. I told her how much I loved Drop Zone.

'You guys helped me in my journey with God,' I said.

'Really?' said Gabby.

'Yeah, you got me thinking about God and then in Year 9 I became a Christian.'

'Wow, you know that's so encouraging. We didn't know if running that program was a waste of time in the end, but if it made a difference in one person's life, it was worth it. You were that one.'

One of the Six

Craig Chapman

Ironically, the statistic first came to my attention just after I received the shattering news of Scotty's death. Not even the scrambled thought process which accompanied that time could lessen its impact. Every day, eight Australians take their own lives. Six of those are men.

I had been chewing this over for a week or so by the time Scotty's eldest son stood up at the funeral to recount some memories of his dad. His reflections included a brief life story written by Scotty himself several years earlier.

The autobiography revealed some facts concerning Scotty's painful journey about which I had somehow remained unaware. Not for the first time, it occurred to me that he had invested more in me over our thirty-seven year friendship than I had in him. His infectious smile and outgoing nature always communicated a heartfelt desire to connect with people. I was typically more withdrawn. I looked around at the mourners, realising how much he had known about my family and how comparatively little I knew of his.

I doubt that any of us were truly surprised to be sitting in that church auditorium at such an event. The warning signs had been flashing for more than two decades. There had been times when he seemed to be doing better. But it was just an illusion. The unrelenting grip of mental illness would not be overcome.

Many had prayed that Scotty's Christian faith would sustain him. He was, after all, unwavering in his conviction that God was with him. Yet I, no doubt along with many others, remained at odds with the final outcome. Where is God in such circumstances?

There was a clarity in Scotty's words as they were read, contrasting sharply with the confusion which had so often characterised him in life. Eventually, the young man who so graphically embodied his father's humble and gracious spirit delivered the kicker.

'Men ... invest in your sons and in each other.'

It felt like a legacy; a prophetic admonition to continue something even though it had ultimately not been enough to save him.

The first time Scotty attempted to end his life completely blindsided me. Our careers had taken us to different parts of the world. I had a wife, young children and a job about which I was passionate. He had those same things and I naively assumed he was as content as I was. I then proceeded to make assumptions about why he did what he did. Only in recent years had I begun to contemplate that my assumptions might be incorrect. The words at his funeral confirmed that this was so. I had spent the better part of twenty years being angry about what he had done without understanding the degree to which his life had spiralled out of control. It was also only more recently that I had been able to look back at the carefree, energetic and popular young man I knew at university and see the signs to which I had remained oblivious at the time.

Though still shocking, the more recent attempts could not truthfully be described as blindsides. They were, however, even more gut-wrenching because of the stark realisation that I could not control what was happening to him. The times I visited him in the mental illness facility at the hospital were difficult and almost unbearably sad. He was in turmoil. He could not accept where he was. There was nothing which could be said to ease his pain or mask the extent to which he had unravelled.

Intermittently, there were some good times. Our hopes were raised each time there appeared to be a turn for the better. Amid stints working overseas, he would often make contact on his return visits. My wife and I loved to have him over for a meal and a catch-up. On one occasion he brought his new Chinese girlfriend. Scotty had acquired a bewildering Chinese accent which seemed to fade in and out. Our neighbour called in unexpectedly with several large blue crabs ready for consumption. Scotty and his companion demolished them whilst continuing to speak what was to us broken-English gibberish. We will never forget that night. I also fondly remember the time I took him to a country football match in which my son was playing. He loved it, roaming the boundary, interacting with other spectators and reminiscing about his own football career. Despite all this, the overall trend continued in a downward spiral.

I had texted him a couple of months before his eventual death. The reply was brief and did not elaborate on how he was going. That was not unusual. I assumed he was still in China and battling on. Unbeknown to me (and many others), he returned to Adelaide and holed himself up in his usual caravan park base. He refused his doctor's advice to go to hospital. He shut himself off, not wanting people to know where he was. The message I received from his ex-wife confirmed that this was where it ended.

So I found myself at my mate's funeral, listening to a young man recite possibly the most honest and vulnerable words his father had ever delivered. A lingering confusion had been simmering within me but the autobiography was like the final piece of an elaborate puzzle. The statement about men needing to invest in each other flicked the switch I had been struggling to find. Somehow, there was some purpose in this senseless waste. I was no less devastated at his loss, but the inner turmoil had been relieved somewhat. The simple words on the card attached to the pamphlet at the funeral service captured it; *Now at peace ...*

I, too, have found some peace in the knowledge that perhaps one of the six Australian men who tragically thought they had no option that day than to end their lives, did not die without purpose. Perhaps, as men look to invest in each other we will come to understand how much God has invested in us. That legacy will continue to drive me.

She Called Me Mouse

Bronwyn Fisher

She calls me Mouse; I look over a few metres to the couch where she is sitting, and our eyes connect. She brings her arms up in front of her, sticks her tongue out and huffs and pants like a dog begging for food. Everyone laughs. She asks me for a cup of coffee. I know how she has it off by heart, by now. She drinks black coffee with no sugar. I always make sure to add a little bit of cold water on the top, so it doesn't burn her mouth.

* * *

My Aunty first nicknamed me Mouse when I was seven. I was a short girl, tiny, with thin ears like a mouse. It was an affectionate nickname. Aunty Chris stayed with us often; I loved it when she visited. She lived down south the other side of town to us. She always kept in touch on the phone; she was on the phone non-stop. When I was young, I only got to talk to family on the phone, so I was always excited to hear from her.

When I was young, we attended church occasionally. When Aunty was staying with us, she would sometimes come to church with us. The church services always seemed to go for a very long time, but we got to go to Sunday School afterwards. It was a traditional Lutheran church with the beautiful long tunes of an organ. One Sunday, Aunty came to church with us. That day at least 3 of us were not paying attention. Dad was bored and was poking me til I giggled. Then he would try to stop me from laughing aloud. I cuddled up to him. Dad stifled his laughter and pointed at Mum, who had Aunty falling asleep on her. Mum discreetly tried to wake my Aunty by poking her. The rest of my family and the people around us were trying not to laugh. I wondered if the pastor could see what was happening, and if he could, I reckon he would have thought it was funny too.

Adventures with her wouldn't always be what other children would call adventures. They were special times. Spontaneous in nature and sometimes quite short; she got tired quickly. Many occasions we caught a bus to the city, although it wasn't far away, it seemed as though it was. We would walk along the river bank, and when she got tired, we would sit down on the grass. She would give me money to go to the shop and get everyone ice cream. If Dad were with us, she would walk into a toy store tell him he needed to buy us all something. Adventures with her were something that we treasured. Now in my memory, I can close my eyes remembering small details of the weather, the food we ate and the places we explored.

Although I didn't understand what was happening at the time, I knew she was a bit different. She could be happy with lots of energy, talkative and not sleep for weeks and then other times she could be depressed and unhappy, resting lots, not eat and hardly talk. Sometimes when these things were happening to her, it got too hard for her to cope; she would then need to stay in hospital. During these times, I would often visit her and gained an understanding of mental health at an early age. Regardless of who the Aunty was in front of me, I loved her. I loved her spontaneity in her manic times and in her low times I hovered nearby wishing I could heal her when she woke up.

As time passed and I got older, I no longer called her Aunty Chris. I called her 'I love Aunty.' When I knew it was her on the phone, I would squeal 'I love Aunty!' loudly so she could hear me. Then I would wait until it was my turn to talk to her. She never liked any of the places I worked, first in aged care and then in mental health care. She worried about me burning out, and she knew the stressors that the health care industry brought and didn't want me to work in that area anymore. It was a constant difference of opinion between us. Despite this, no matter what mood she was in, no matter how much other people felt irritated with her; I refused to view her negatively. I knew in my heart that she acted the way she did because she cared a lot.

The phone call to make me fearful of all future phone calls occurred. One evening I'm excitedly unpacking parcels that would remain on my table for weeks. I received the worst news that my Aunty had died suddenly. I didn't just go into shock; I felt all the stages of grief in an instant. While the pain settled in my body and mind, all the grief I had ever felt consolidated to one. I crumbled inwardly, and I expressed my anger and sadness outwardly. How could this happen? How could I come to terms with the fact that I would never be able to talk to her again, never get to ask her for advice, never get to ask her questions that came to mind? I even despaired that I would never argue with her again. She always spoke her mind, always spoke on the phone for hours and was more loyal than anyone you will ever meet.

My emotions were all over the place. Sleepless nights became the new normal for me. Everywhere I went, I would see women with the same type of appearance and think it was her. My faith hadn't changed, but I wondered a lot if God knew that I was hurting and how much? Did God know I just needed to see her? Why did it happen now? The last time I spoke to her, she was telling me my job was too stressful, and I needed to quit. I was annoyed with her but didn't say anything.

I attended every service we had at my church for months after she passed away, seeking solace. I felt supported by everyone who knew what had happened. My church played all the Hillsong songs that I had come to love. I feigned heartfelt worship and devotion at church. I never had to fake love for God, that never left me, but all I felt was emptiness. I had many questions for God, and I had many prayers that I spoke to God.

It took months to feel anything except for deep, harrowing grief. Slowly the intensity of the pain lessened. I couldn't have gotten through it without the love of friends, my church and the love of God. Something that I still remember strongly was that the humanness in Jesus became very real to me. It was a comfort to me that Jesus also went through grief; therefore, he *understands* what I'm going through. It began to strengthen within me the understanding that Jesus has human emotions. Jesus felt sadness and anger. At the same time, I also felt a deeper understanding of God's love for all people, and that includes me at all times.

From time to time, I have longings to see her. I wish she could see me get married and have children. I long to ask her advice even though I didn't always agree with it. As I keep moving forward, I am continually comforted by God's love. I am thankful that God gave someone to me that I hold dear to my heart, including the memories of the times she called me Mouse.

On My Dirty Knees
Sally Shaw

The opportune moment to attack had arrived. From a dormant state, they had surreptitiously multiplied with relentless determination and prolific seed production. Now nothing deterred them. They were fearless, with no respect for anything in their way. The indigenous grasses and bushes tried to fight back but, in the end, gave up. Those they conquered included the local butterflies and moths who depended on the rich nectar of the indigenous plants.

These invaders had been introduced by early settlers whose imported cattle could only thrive, they thought, on grass from the motherland. But today in the Adelaide Hills where I live, they were an invasive plant, a declared weed.

I stood and contemplated what lay ahead. My unwelcome invaders with their dense tufts of spidery light green leaves were oblivious to my presence. A nearby kookaburra laughed. I agreed with it, my task was ridiculous. Despite this, I carefully triaged the different tufts, some small, others large, to decide which could be quickly removed. I imagined myself putting on a surgical hat as I picked up the trowel with its sharp metal ridges. A ray of sun reflected glimmers of light from its surface causing a momentary blinding glare. I blinked a couple of times and reminded myself of the surgical operation ahead. I fell onto my knees, not in an act of adoration, but as a commando eager to overwhelm and destroy my enemy.

I lifted the trowel, now a commando's knife, and plunged it deep into the side of the thick turf. As I stabbed again and again, I imagined cries of protest, followed by screams of agony.

I directed the knife towards the turf's epicentre. My hand ached and my knees felt damp from the moist soil. For a moment, I was a noble Desert Father with a commitment to austerity, sacrifice and prayer. But there was nothing saintly about my work as I earnestly sought to defeat the invader. Perhaps though it was a prayer of intercession, of lament for an environment now in deep crisis, crying out for release from human oppression.

I breathed deeply and paused to wipe away the beads of sweat that now dripped into my eyes. I needed to see clearly so the final stage of my operation would be successful. As I plunged again, I sensed my enemy's tight grip was failing. I threw down the trowel and grabbed the thick turf. It moved. One more yank. Its power had gone, and I pulled it out with a shout of victory. I held it up with its thick roots caked in soil and glared at it.

'You don't belong here so I'm getting rid of you!'

I casually tossed it into a nearby bucket; it thumped heavily as it landed causing the bucket to shudder. As I stood up to relieve my aching legs, I looked down to the gaping hole. Another bead of sweat fell into my eyes, and I wiped it away and blinked again. At that moment my eyes opened wide and my mouth fell open. I was an excited child who had discovered a secret.

'Wow! That's incredible,' I gasped.

Right next to the hole a small delicate-looking bush with green, nearly cylindrical leaves spiked at the ends was revealed. On display among them were yellow star-like flowers. I fell to my knees to examine it closely.

'How could such a delicate plant thrive under the threatening tendrils of a large clump of invasive grass?'

Now, instead of drops of sweat, my eyes were full of tears - tears of joy and amazement.

'You're so gorgeous,' I whispered.

I don't often hear God's voice, but at that moment I distinctly heard a message:

These invasive weeds represent the destructive practices that have occurred in Australia since the settlers arrived. As a result, my creation has been oppressed, invaded and destroyed. It is struggling to survive but I haven't given up on it. I love it and will continue to sustain it, just like this little Prickly Guinea flower, (for that is what I later learnt it was). *I want you to speak and act against this injustice. The world needs to hear this vital message.*

'Oh my, this is such an important message,' I gasped.

I felt like Moses, so inadequately prepared. I didn't have the right qualifications or status to give me any credibility. This calling was clear, but like Moses, I started to doubt and make excuses.

'How can I discern God's direction?'

As I tried to work out what to do, I felt bewildered. Why do so many Christians I talk to refuse to engage in this topic or just give me a blank stare? Surely, they know that God wants us to look after his creation?

I considered for a moment the life of Moses and other Old Testament prophets. It was not easy for them. They were mocked and misunderstood. They didn't have academic qualifications, but they did soak themselves in God's word.

This was an 'AHA!' moment as I realised I too had an opportunity to immerse myself in God's word. I enrolled in a Diploma in Theology program, which later led to a Master of Ministry, with a focus on the biblical basis for creation care, known as eco-theology. These studies expanded the understanding I had that caring for God's creation was a vital part of the Christian life. I realised that God the Creator has redeemed not just humans, but all he has made.

I remembered a Christian friend who had told me, after I'd tried to explain my desire to see all Christians involved in caring for God's creation, 'I love praising God for his amazing creation but as Jesus is returning soon it's more important to be saving souls.'

I tried to explain what I'd learnt but made no progress. She was not interested.

My heart sank. 'What else could I do? Having more biblical knowledge didn't seem to help. Perhaps if I found a Christian organisation that did conservation work, I could invite my friends to join me. 'After all, it was when I was digging up weeds that I had my revelation,' I muttered

Some internet searching led me to *A Rocha*, a Christian organisation with conservation projects in a number of countries around the world. I was impressed by their five values: Christian, Conservation, Community, Cooperation and Cross-cultural. *A Rocha* means 'the rock' in Portuguese, as their first project started in Portugal. At that time, they did not have a formal organisation in Australia, but by 2016 they did – and I became one of their directors!

Surely this had fulfilled my calling? I wondered. *A Rocha Australia* had so much to offer Christians: practical care for God's amazing creation.

I tried to encourage my friend to join in some of our activities.

'Sally, you might enjoy digging, weeding, revegetating, but that's the last thing I want to do,' she retorted.

I realised that many modern-day prophets, like the biblical prophets, want to give up their difficult call. But they remarkably persist as they dig deeper into God's word and pray more in order to overcome the opposition. I also needed to do this. I needed God's wisdom – and it came a little later.

'Sally, you're an educator with experience in improvisational drama, why don't you use those skills?' my husband commented one day. He had sensed my disappointment.

Another 'AHA!' moment. Yes, I could design and implement a series of experiential arts-based workshops where the participants could explore in creative ways the biblical reasons why Christians are called to care for God's creation.

My heartrate increased as I contemplated this possibility. Was this to be the final part of my calling? Could it be a way to encourage Christians to care for and restore God's hurting creation – human and non-human? It is not just Prickly Guinea-flowers that need help, but vast numbers of other species that are being undermined by enemy onslaughts. We as Christians must respond to God's call to overcome the invaders. It is an urgent call.

I Like Boys
Jane Walker

'I like boys,' Haru said, ducking his head so I could not see his eyes.

I took in a deep breath. For Haru, as a young Japanese man in the 1990s, same sex attraction was a huge problem, something disgraceful. His path in life had already been laid out by his parents and society – university, job, marriage, children. He didn't want to be different from any other Japanese, so he tried to hide it.

As a naïve country girl with little understanding of homosexuality, I didn't know how to respond. All I knew was that everyone comes to God in the same way – through faith in Christ and no problem was too big for God to handle. I also felt a genuine God-given sisterly love for Haru and 'adopted' him as my little brother, introducing him to people that way. They would look very puzzled, their eyes going back and forth from me, a bespectacled Australian girl and short Haru with his spiky, dyed brown hair and fashionable clothes.

As we met up in cafes to drink coffee, Haru would often complain to me about his troubles. One day I got tired of just listening. I wrote down all his problems on a serviette and said I would pray for them right then and there. Even though he was an atheist and we were in public, Haru respectfully listened. After that, I would often pray when we hung out and eventually Haru began praying too.

I invited him to a Christian young adults outreach group I was a helper in. It was lightly evangelistic and big on fun and laughter. Haru became a regular attender.

Throughout this time Haru would often ask questions about God and faith. For him, a huge stumbling block was his same sex attraction. If he became a Christian, what would God require him to do? Would God take his attractions away? Would he become 'straight'? Was that even what he really wanted?

Amidst all this wrestling, Haru heard about a conference run in America for Christians struggling with their sexuality and he very much wanted to go. There were a few problems with this – it was far away, it was all in English and it was expensive. He worried that he wouldn't be able to understand it enough to participate and that he wouldn't be able to connect naturally with the other participants. He wanted me to come with him. I didn't really have the money, but took on an extra job, working long hours to raise the funds.

I'd just got enough money to pay for the conference when the leader of the young adults group contacted me to say she was worried about Haru. He seemed to be such a teachable, easily influenced person. Why wasn't he becoming a Christian? She decided Haru needed to spend time with some Japanese Christians who were primed to share the gospel with him and she arranged for Haru to stay with these friends of hers right after the conference.

Haru and I both found the conference an extraordinary experience. For the first time Haru walked around in a crowd of strangers who knew his secret and did not reject him for it. He could be completely honest. Haru had always shied away from talking to foreign young men because he felt uncomfortable around them; now he felt accepted by them. I had grown up in church circles, but I had never been to a Christian gathering like this, where people were so real and humble about their brokenness and so loving, supportive and welcoming of others. Being there felt like meeting Jesus.

Haru said his heart opened like a flower to God for the first time at the conference.

Afterwards, he went and stayed with our leader's friends who pressured him to become a Christian until his heart closed again to God. He felt bullied by the experience. His conclusion was this: the conference was amazing, but Christians aren't like that in real life and I remembered how even in our young adults group, some of the Christian leaders would make gay jokes or put down gay people.

It was at that point that I prayed the most bizarre prayer I've ever prayed. I asked God to help me find a group of Christians who would accept Haru for who he was and where he was at.

That very Sunday after I'd prayed, Haru and I decided to try out a new quite conservative church. We arrived and were faced with a sudden choice. Go to church first, then Sunday School (classes for adults) or vice versa. We chose church first, then randomly picked a Sunday School class.

There were three young men in the room and two girls. After the class, the five of them invited us to lunch. I discovered they all had paid jobs as singers, dancers and actors at two well-known local attractions that had musical acts. Despite Haru's initial awkwardness around the guys, we straight away became friends, hanging out with them after church and on weekends.

This instant friendship group was clearly a gift from God. As we enjoyed their company, I had the recurring sense that there was a reason why Haru was so accepted.

When two of the guys were due to leave to return home, Haru and I went to visit them to say goodbye and our story spilled out: where Haru was at; what we prayed. And I found out how fully God had answered my prayer. Two of the boys were at a similar place – trying to work out how to deal with their same-sex attractions in the context of their faith.

Not long after this, Haru and I were praying about another situation. Afterwards he confidently said, 'God will answer. He always does'. I was astounded. How had he moved from atheism to such a strong belief in a God who listened and cared for him? Only by praying sincere impossible prayers and seeing God so graciously respond.

He is Alone

Rosalind Lum

In March 1961, mum discovered that she was pregnant with her seventh child and the news spread to our neighbours. The couple living next door asked my parents whether they could adopt their unborn child. 'It does not matter whether the child is a girl or a boy', they said. The couple had married at an older age and could not have children of their own.

My parents found themselves in a dilemma; should they bless this childless couple with their precious child or keep this child and struggle even more financially?

Eventually, my parents gave in to compassion. So, they blessed this couple with a beautiful baby boy. A precious gift from God.

Soon after adopting their baby son, the couple next door moved away without leaving their contact details. It must have been heartbreaking for my parents to see them go. They were resigned to not seeing their son again. However, he was not forgotten and remained treasured in their hearts.

In 1963, mum fell pregnant with her 8th child. It was a boy again, a blessing from God. God was able to heal the heartache my parents experienced from the separation from their seventh child.

Out of the blue in 2017, I was reminded of my younger brother who had been given up for adoption. I was moved to tears each time I thought of him. These words 'He is alone and you have seven of you' kept ringing in my ears.

'Why now?' I asked myself. I vaguely remembered he was adopted, as I was only seven years old at the time. I had never thought of my younger brother all these years, let alone to look for him.

'But why was my brother alone?' I asked myself. I presumed he would be married with children.

After several more emotional breakdowns I realised that the Holy Spirit was trying to attract my attention. God kept stirring my heart through waves of sadness. He was reminding me that my younger brother was alone and I should look for him.

'But how?' I thought. It was like looking for a needle in a haystack. So, I put the matter in the too hard basket.

Nevertheless, I started praying to God to stir my brother's heart that he would like to know his biological family.

God would not let me give up. Again, in the early morning of August 19, 2018, I was reminded of my younger brother. 'He is alone and you have seven of you', God repeated over and over again. Shortly thereafter the Holy Spirit overcame me with indescribable emotions and I burst into a flood of tears.

I knew I had to pay serious attention to God's prompting this time.

The search

With obedience, I contacted my siblings in Singapore about my intentions to look for our brother and to seek their help.

We started by searching on social media but did not find a match. I decided to make it my mission to find my brother during my trip to Singapore planned for March 2019.

I continued to pray to God. I asked that if it is his will, to give me the courage to search for my brother. Most importantly, I asked God to lead me to the right contacts to help me on my search.

I prayed to God to help find my brother before mum's 90th birthday which was coming up on March 30, 2019. It would be the best birthday present for mum.

Just before departing for Singapore, I received news from my youngest brother. He had spoken to his circle of church friends about our intentions to look for our brother. One brother in Christ quietly offered to help us with our search. I believe God planted this godly person among my brother's friends with intentions to use him to accomplish God's work.

A week later, the search for our brother commenced and it was only a matter of time now until we found him.

Mum's 90th birthday celebration arrived and there was still no news of our brother. Surprisingly, I was not disappointed. We had a big surprise birthday party for mum, full of fun and laughter and everyone had a wonderful time.

I believed it was not meant to be. I knew that God's plan is not our plan. His timing is always right. We must put our trust in God.

If it was God's will to reunite Mum and her son and his siblings, he would make it happen, through ways beyond our imagination.

The breakthrough

On April 11, 2019 we were elated to receive news that our brother had been located. He was eager to meet his mother and provided his telephone number.

With a thankful heart, I contacted my brother and we organised to meet at McDonald's the next day.

Accompanied by my brother Jim and sister Julia, my heart raced as we headed towards the meeting location. So many questions crossed my mind. I just wanted to know whether 'He is alone'.

As we waited inside of McDonalds, an inquisitive face appeared through the window. I immediately recognised him as our brother. He closely resembled my eldest brother.

My newly found brother introduced himself as Patrick.

Patrick came across as an easy going guy. We talked about our families and showed him photos of mum taken at her 90th birthday party. Patrick said he only wished we had found him earlier; he would love to have celebrated mum's birthday with us.

Patrick's father passed away 30 years ago and his mother recently passed away in September 2017 at 90 years old. His parents never mentioned he was adopted. He only found out after his adopted mother died and he discovered a copy of his birth certificate with his biological parents name on it.

I was so anxious to ask the question that had been playing on my mind. 'Are you married Patrick?' I asked. 'No', he answered. 'I am now alone after mum passed away. She was living with me all these years'.

With tears in my eyes, I told Patrick that God knew him so well, well before we did. I shared with him my encounter with God and how God had been constantly reminding me that he was alone ever since his adopted mother passed away in 2017.

Unfortunately, I had to return to Australia for other commitments and we had to postpone the reunion of mother and son to the following month.

Good news

On May 26, 2019, I returned to Singapore to reunite my mother and her son after almost 58 years apart.

'Mum, we recently found your second youngest son, Patrick', I said. We all smiled and awaited a happy response. Instead mum became upset. 'Why? Why did you find him?' she replied as she choked back tears.

I explained that we wanted to reunite her with her son and that Patrick was eager to meet his biological mother.

Mum continued to shake her head and tearfully said 'I can't. I can't. I did not raise him. I am not worthy to be his mother'.

I reminded mum that her kindness and compassion blessed a childless couple with a precious son.

I explained God had found him and wanted to bless her and reunite her with her son. I shared with her my encounter with the Holy Spirit and how God revealed to me that her son was alone.

Eventually, we convinced mum to accept Patrick as her son and to welcome him into our family.

The reunion dinner

Patrick appeared very composed as he entered the dining room. Patrick placed his arm around mum's shoulder and called her 'Ah Mah' ('Mother' in Hokkien dialect). He asked how she was and told mum she looked so well. Patrick was all smiles. Mum tried to be strong and smiled back. It did not take long for mum to warm up to her son.

He is Alone

Patrick and mum compared their birth certificates and adoption papers. Many questions were exchanged. Stories were shared and lots of laughter ensued.

It was a perfect night filled with cherished memories. I felt God's presence throughout the entire evening.

Patrick went home and realised the immensity of this life changing event. He had gone from being 'alone' to having fifty-three new family members: a mother, four brothers, three sisters and their spouses, twenty nieces and nephews, and twenty great nieces and nephews.

Patrick messaged my brother Jim and said, 'I was so happy to meet mum last night. I am crying right now.' I only wished I was there to give him a hug.

More Than a Piece of Paper
Hannah Matthews

I remember when I was nine years old. I was standing next to my mother in the neonatal ICU just a few days after she had given birth to my twin brothers, while she is bathing the youngest baby out of my newborn twin brothers and said to her, 'Mum when I grow up I want to be a nurse, I want to be a nursery nurse'. I had no idea what that meant. I just knew from that moment on, I wanted to become a nurse when I grew up.

This was the start to a very long and distant dream that as a child, I wanted so desperately but felt that I could never achieve. Throughout my life, I had experienced a lot of disappointment and heartache and lack of support. I grew up in the Northern Territory and moved to South Australia at the age of nine only three months after my twin brothers were born. I had to leave all my friends and start afresh in a new state and a new school.

Much of my childhood is very vague. A lot of my memory has been suppressed as I was sexually abused as a young child by my father. My insecurities, lack of self-belief and lack of confidence have always been a strong part of who I am. I grew up not only being sexually abused but also mentally abused, being told I'm overweight and called many names. This took its toll as a young girl who just wanted to become a nurse.

When I was in year 7, my mum enrolled me into St Johns first aid, and I loved it. I started to feel like my dreams of becoming a nurse might just be reachable. Then came high school and year 11. Year 11 was when my life started to spiral down. It was the year I started to have nightmares about my childhood. Year 11 was the year the truth came out about being sexually abused by my father. I had to move out of home at the age of 15, and for some reason, it was up to me whether I pressed charges against my father, and I was worried about where my mother and siblings would live. I moved in with one of my aunties. I felt like everyone knew about my situation at school and felt uncomfortable, so halfway through year 11, I moved schools. I ended up moving to five different houses in year 12. Even though I passed year 12, I got a measly 40 for my TER score and required an average of 60 to get into nursing. My dream of becoming a nurse went out of the window.

Four years later, my Grandad was diagnosed with pancreatic cancer, and I remember taking my Nanna to and from the aged care home to visit him, and my heart started longing to become a nurse again. Someone mentioned to me that I don't have to go to university to become a nurse, I could do enrolled nursing at TAFE. All my life my Grandad has asked me what I wanted to do with my life, and I couldn't answer him. I received an offer into TAFE in December 2013. I finally had an answer to his question, but I could no longer tell him as he died in October of that year.

My final placement came in September 2015, and I remember finding it hard because I was so close to reaching that dream. I was in the middle of a six-week placement and had a mental breakdown. I couldn't cope with the pressure of being a student nurse, being a girlfriend, and maintaining a house. I decided that I needed help and went and spoke to my doctor and told him I needed to go on antidepressants. I wasn't coping. He was reluctant to put me on them but decided to listen and put me on the lowest dose. I thought this would solve all my problems, but ultimately, it was just a Band-Aid to my wounds. I remember not being able to cry and just feeling numb and thought I can't be a nurse that feels nothing. After a month, I stopped taking the medication. October 2015 came, and before I knew it, I had finished TAFE and was officially an Enrolled Nurse, I started my first job in November 2015.

Even though I was an Enrolled Nurse, I still felt like something deep within was missing, and for a long time, I was debating if I wanted to go to university to become a Registered Nurse. I still had those negative thoughts about not being smart enough for university. One night I decided to bite the bullet and apply. I thought, what do I have to lose?

In 2017 I started university to become a Registered Nurse. In my first year, we had to do something called an OSCA (objective structured clinical assessment). I remember having done one which involved infants and maths calculations for medication, and as soon as I hear the word 'maths', I freak out. I remember going into my OSCA and doing everything I needed correctly until the maths, I had 5 minutes to work out the medication calculation, and my mind froze. I panicked and couldn't do the calculation. The time went, and I just started crying and walked outside. My tutor was there and asked if I was okay. I responded, 'I failed; I know I have failed.' My tutor said to me, 'You don't know if you have yet'. A few weeks later, the results came out and by the grace of God I had passed. As part of that subject, students were required to do an online certificate which included ten marks for the OSCA and that ten marks had brought my overall score to 51. I had passed by one mark.

My second year of nursing was extremely hard, especially with having to work and study full time and do a placement. I shed many tears, and on my final placement, we received our results for our second to last assignment, which I failed by three marks. This subject was the last I needed to complete to receive my degree. I remember finding out while I was on shift and I couldn't eat, I couldn't focus. I was at lunch and had to walk away and have a cry. This broke me once again; I thought, I was never going to become a Registered Nurse. I felt ripped off and almost went for a re-mark because I felt like I was being hard done by.

I decided to work harder on my final assignment because ultimately getting my bachelor's degree came down to that last assignment. I stayed up late because I had no time during the day with placement and work to be able to complete this assignment. I even took the day off that it was due, and I uploaded it six times because I kept changing things.

A few weeks later, the results were released. I had finished an early shift, and my phone was going flat so I went home put it on charge and fell asleep and woke up to the email that the results were available. I sat there for about five minutes to scared to open the email to see what result I got. I took in some deep breaths and opened the link to see that I had received a credit. I had passed the subject!

More Than a Piece of Paper

In April 2019 I was able to walk on stage and receive my Bachelor of Nursing degree, something that nine-year-old me had planted in her heart and teenage me never thought was possible. By the grace of God I was able to overcome what had happened to me as a child. Without my faith and strength, I would not be the caring and compassionate nurse I am today. This is why my bachelor's degree is more than a piece of paper. It represents endurance, hope, and transformation.

Arise

Claire-Louise Watson

I sit cross-legged on the rug, and stare at the book in the Sunday School teacher's hand.

She holds it high so we can see the pictures. 'Jairus' daughter was very sick, so he went to ask Jesus for help.'

I look at the girl in the picture. I know she is much older than me, because her feet almost touch the end of the bed. The girl is asleep but her mother looks worried, like my own mother did when I jumped off a chest of drawers when I was two. I bit my tongue when I landed and it had to be stitched by the doctor. There is another man in the picture too, but I recognise him: his name is Jesus. He appears in many of the stories at Sunday School. One week he gave sight to a man who was blind, and the next he gave strength to a man who couldn't walk. The strangest stories about him are told at Easter-time, when the teacher describes his death on a cross. I do not like that story, even though it has a happy ending when he is raised from the dead three days later. I know lots of stories about Jesus, but I do not know him. Not like I know my mother's smile, or the voice of my father singing 'Little house upon the lake' when I can't sleep, or the footholds in the branches of the tree in our front garden. He is a faraway God who belongs to another place and time.

The teacher turns the page. 'While Jairus was waiting for Jesus, his servants came and told him: 'Your daughter is dead. Don't bother Jesus anymore.' But Jesus told him not to be afraid. 'Just believe.'

I don't understand what it means to die. I have seen dead snails in the garden, but I have never seen a dead person. I look at my best friend beside me, and wonder if she could come over to play after lunch. The sun is shining through the window; it creates patterns on the rug and makes my friend's black hair gleam. I turn back to the book and see Jesus reach a hand towards the girl.

The teacher smiles. 'Jesus said: "Little girl, arise." The girl got up, and Jesus gave her back to her parents. He told them to give her something to eat.'

It seems less impressive than last week's story, when Jesus fed a huge crowd with just five loaves of bread and two fish. I have learnt enough maths to know that five plus two does not equal five thousand meals. But the parents of the girl look happy she is awake again. I wriggle around on the mat and wait for the teacher to explain the craft activity.

Thirty years later, I sit on the couch with our youngest child in my arms and my husband by my side. Hannah had been discharged from hospital the previous day.

'There's nothing else we can do,' the doctors had said. 'You can take her home.'

Like Jairus I have been to see Jesus about Hannah, not once but countless times. For I know Jesus now. I know him better than my mother's smile, and his voice is more familiar than my father's. His words are like the footholds in the tree I once climbed: they guide my steps.

Hannah's cheeks were pink when we left, but now they are an ominous grey, like clouds before a storm. Her eyes are shut and her breathing is noisy. She has not moved all morning, nor can she. The disease has sapped every last ounce of her energy, and she is no longer able to eat or drink. Earlier that morning, she had ceased breathing for a moment. Yet she does not appear in any distress, and the palliative care nurse who visited earlier remarked on how peaceful she looked.

Outside the window the thoughtless sun is shining, and the autumn colours glow with beauty. In the distance I hear the faint sound of the school bell, which signals the beginning of recess. I imagine the children streaming out of the classrooms, with boundless energy and squeals of laughter. It is a day for living, not for dying.

While we are sitting on the couch, Hannah takes another long pause in her breathing. The seconds feel like hours as I wait for her to breathe again.

'We love you, Hannah. You're a wonderful daughter,' I say.

Her legs stiffen and the strength of the muscle contraction surprises me, since I have not witnessed any movement in her limbs since the previous day. Then her back arches as if she is a limp puppet being lifted by a string.

'Are you stretching, Hannah?' I ask.

It suddenly dawns on me what is happening. The room becomes silent, and the colour drains from her blue lips.

Then we weep. Weep for the child who was, and weep for the young woman who might have been, and weep for ourselves and our sons. When my husband has finished weeping, he gets up from the couch.

'I'll sit and hold her for a while,' I say. It no longer seems right to use her name, for the Hannah I knew has gone.

He nods, for there are no more words to say.

I shut my eyes so I cannot see her still grey face, and imagine instead the expectant face of Jairus as he stood beside his daughter's bed. I see Jesus take her hand and call her name, Talitha. Her cheeks become rosy, like the first blush of sunrise. I pray to Jesus to do the same for Hannah. When I open my eyes I stare at the cold body in my arms. I get up from the couch and place it in the cot.

Five years later, on the anniversary of her death, I sit in the garden where Hannah's ashes are buried. Pink blossoms cover the bottlebrush tree my parents-in-law planted to mark the spot. The Bible is in my hands, and I read once more of Jairus and his daughter. The story is so familiar I know it by heart, yet as I read God reveals a new insight: the words Jesus spoke to Talitha are the same he spoke to my daughter. My ears could not discern his voice, but Hannah heard him: 'Little girl, arise.'

Out of My Depth

Teri Kempe

As I sat in the principal's office something caught my eye outside. A man was coming down the muddy path in the rain. He seemed anxious, even distressed.

'Excuse me, sir, who is that man outside?' I asked.

The principal strained to see through the fogged up window. 'It looks a lot like Leah's dad,' he said.

He left the room. Soon a runner was sent to find Leah, a Fifth Form student.

I watched as Leah ran to her father, they embraced and cried together. I had been living in Fiji for about six months as an Australian pensioner volunteering at a mission school just outside the capital, Suva. Coming from Australia I was used to my diary, set times and well-planned days. This all went out the window in Fiji. Each day was a challenge and I never knew what might happen next.

About twenty minutes later the principal returned to his office and explained the situation.

'Leah's mum passed away some time last year and her dad blamed himself because he wasn't there when she died. If he could have taken his wife to hospital for treatment, she wouldn't have died. The dad, Joseph, completely lost it. He was consumed with guilt and grief. He had not seen Leah for six months and had been sleeping on a park bench.'

'What can we do to help them?' I ventured.

'Well, now that they have found each other, it's important they stay together. What do you think? Would you be able to help them? It would only be for a short time until they find a home.'

I was renting a three bedroom apartment, and at the time had two bedrooms free. I put myself in their shoes and knew what I had to do, though two strangers coming to live in my home was daunting. Before we left the school that day, Principal Malak invited us to share tea and we all prayed together.

We left by taxi for my home. Joseph and Leah came with only a few clothes. Some friends kindly visited with food for us. We again spent time in prayer, singing and praising God and enjoyed our first meal together.

When the visitors left, Joseph and Leah settled into their room with hardly a word. Joseph could not look at me. He seemed to be on autopilot, barely conscious of what was happening around him. His daughter, aged around fifteen, was overjoyed to see him and so grateful for a place to sleep. The first few days were awkward, with little meaningful conversation. I did not have a car, so I took Leah to school by taxi, or we caught the bus. Joseph stayed home and I wondered what he would do all day.

I was pleasantly surprised to come home one day to find Joseph had dug up the back garden ready to plant some vegetables. He had found a spade in the back shed and the effort seemed to encourage him.

After a few weeks I learned there were other, older, children in the family whom they had lost touch with. First, there was Leah's older sister, Grace, who had finished school and was working. The grapevine works well in Suva and Joseph was able to locate her living with some friends. It was a great reunion when Grace joined us for dinner one night. Her living arrangement was not good, so it was not long before she moved in with us too.

Next, I learnt there was a brother, James. He had also left school and was squatting with some friends and apparently living aimlessly. After some time he came to live with us as well. James was a good musician and loved to strum his guitar and sing gospel songs. It brought both peace and joy to the household. Sometimes James and Joseph even sang together. Both James and Grace were somewhat itinerant, coming and going as they pleased. I was never quite sure when they would be home.

Many nights I was working late at the school or had meetings for the various groups I supported so the reunited family had the home to themselves. They cooked and cleaned and generally looked after themselves. Whenever we could we shared devotions and prayers, as I encouraged them to have a positive outlook and trust God to take care of their needs.

Although Joseph applied for assisted housing it was declined. He was advised it was only available to single mums with young children, not single dads. So, as Joseph did not yet have regular work, the chances of them finding their own home seemed remote.

I was grateful my Australian pension came at a favourable exchange rate, and with the cost of living low, I could manage to support them. We lived very simply with few modern conveniences, but we were safe and dry, and gradually hope was being restored.

There were always challenges for students at school. Principal Malak was principal, counsellor and pastor to the students – but more than that, many of them called him 'Dad'. He took a deep interest in their personal wellbeing, often visiting the families of troubled students to find the root cause and offer support. He and his wife had, through the years, taken many into their own home, despite having six children of their own.

Over the next few years several other students were added to our 'family'. Tevita was homeless, a university dropout with a traumatic childhood, who Principal Malak had previously rescued and supported through high school. He decided to return to school to improve his marks and try for university again. He was a delight to have with us. He was compassionate and kind and ever-willing to help with everything around the home. We spent many hours singing, praying and sharing the Word together. He not only worked hard himself but helped and encouraged the others.

One day Principal Malak found a suicide note. Fortunately he was not too late and the troubled young student, Stephen, who was being abused at home, received counselling and prayer. But now he was homeless, so with only a change of clothes and a few school books, he joined our family too.

Later a female student, truanting from another school and a runaway, found her way to our school. She moved in with us. It was hard for her to settle and she was the most challenging. I was not sure she was telling the truth as her story didn't quite add up.

She stayed on and off. She later told friends I had deeply influenced her for good, but it certainly did not seem like it at the time.

By this time my linen supply had been all but exhausted and my bank balance was low. How could I help find bedding for yet another desperate young person? Completely unexpectedly, there was a knock on my door.

'My sister is returning to America and she heard you had quite a household here. She asked me to give you these', said the stranger standing there. This wonderful lady then brought huge sacks of new bedding – sheets, pillowcases, doonas, towels and pillows. There was enough and to spare. Each item was still in its original wrapping. We could only thank and praise God for this wonderful unexpected provision.

Each new family member stretched us all, but somehow, with God's help, and encouragement from the Principal and other teachers, we stumbled along. It was a steep learning curve for me and many times I felt completely out of my depth. I now had a 'family' of seven living with me. The girls were in one room, the boys in another and Joseph slept in the lounge, as he often went to bed late. Thankfully I had my own room and bathroom, to which I could retreat.

As I look back on the four years of 'house guests' who became family, it is amazing to see how God enabled us to live together and grow in grace. There were many times when I wept for them as they made poor choices, but there were equally many times when we laughed, sang, worshipped and prayed together. Each has found their own way now and I don't know what the future holds for them. I only know it was a very special time, and God has them in his care.

Son of Man
al Bikaadi

I'm a *gubba*, a white fella. Aunty says my mob came from outer space, that blackfellas are connected to the earth but we are not. I don't understand.

'We feel the unconditional love,' she says. 'Your mob are aliens. You aren't connected. Go take a walk in the bush. Lie down on the grass and look at the stars. Your lot need to understand that you're being watched. The ancestors are right beside us all the time.'

My first vivid memory is seeing my mother drive away. A blonde, bronzed boy was I, with flowers in my hand for a ghost. Nanna tried to put me in a boy's home, but mum got me back. She hadn't died in the accident but her mind was elsewhere for years. So I was alone.

I was alone in the backstreets of Enmore's shopfronts. There I had to do illicit stuff to feel safer – safer from the addicts and drag queens that shared our accommodation. I was alone on the fields of Waterloo, between the blocks of Redfern, where dysfunctional families smashed their humanity into further fragments. I was alone when mum married a man who could never be a father to me. Alone, when he overdosed and joined the other dead.

In 1987 we left Elsie's women's refuge to live in Harris Park. A women's refuge was a place where women at risk and their children could find safety and support. In eel country, I was isolated as well. I grew up on the edge of a patchy multiculturalism, but I was always outside all – growing crooked. I had no identity. Neither 'son', nor 'male', nor 'Australian'. I don't recall anything about whiteness. 'Blackfella' was a funny term that didn't mean much, like 'Homeboy' or 'Bomber'. The 'N' word was just part of a pop-band name. American music was a useful vent but I was truly colour blind: Jacko's later assertion that 'it doesn't matter' would have been a non-statement to me. My first girlfriend was Cook Islander, her skin was just part of her – no history there. My best friend was Aboriginal but I didn't really know him. We just survived together, worked out how to eat free of charge. Then we lost contact. Once I felt so alone I drank a laboratory. The convulsions weren't pleasant. Hospital was humiliating. I didn't die.

In 1990 I was somewhere else. A foster mother took me in. She saw my 'whiteness' but she loved me anyway. Middle Eastern mumma ruled the house as queen. I wanted out, but 'pigs' were about and 'custody of the state' could be a fatal hex. I cried.

She told me about Jesus.

'Don't need any of that religion stuff,' I said.

But the Christian school was our last option: a place of too many 'goodie-two-shoes' that had no idea what a West Coast cooler was, and thought 'smoking' was from the *mooglies,* the demons. Funny thing is, eventually, I came to see that life was bigger than me. You might call it 'reverse' peer pressure.

On a wet January in southern New South Wales, I was lost and threatened with extinction. I had nowhere else to go but up or down. What followed was nothing less than a regeneration, signified by a follow-up dunking. Jesus brought me peace. A few months later, I offered myself to God, and to love my birth mother according to the commandments. The reunion brought us to 'Auburnon' in an emerging Qur'an belt – Lebanese, Turk and South Asian families left and right. Colour became everything. It became the bridge to 'know one another'. I sang Anglican chants in Telegu and learnt an Islamic prayer. I threw my knives and forks away. Carpets and curries swallowed me into a place of acceptance I had never before known.

Aunty says I was lucky. 'That Duck Creek is a bora site of healing. The ancestors were helping ya.'

The tranquillity was a balm for our sore souls, Mum and me. True.

Then a fire was briefly kindled by the Toronto Revival, which puffed spirit upon the Great South Land via Randwick Baptist Church. I felt anointed, and tasted the goodness of the Lord again. Stagnation of the soul around 1995 didn't last long, as I came across a Jamaican-looking Sri Lankan-Australian youth pastor. That was where I learnt that I was 'a young person' with 'rights' and acquired a sense of empowerment. Through his Pentecostal church and friends at work, I soon found myself immersed in more culture. By 2000, I was part of the furniture in Sydney's Indonesian community – before it became divided by religious politics. We were all somewhat ecumenical back then. We knew how to be mutually human: Muslims, Hindus, Buddhists, and Christians living side by side (*Bhinneka Tunggal Ika* – Out of Many, One – the national motto of Indonesia).

2001 and 2002 changed our world forever. Trust broke down. Relationships soured. Australia went dark. By 2004 I was planning my exit. In 2006 I bailed. I immersed myself in the Arab Gulf parallel universe. It felt like the 'Auburnon' I'd left behind but on steroids – Jeddah meets New York. The merging of Bedouin culture with urbanisation and international cosmopolitan markets in the UAE was the perfect fit for my already well-stretched heart.

Over the years, I have been carried to offbeat countries like Yemen, Bangladesh, and Pakistan. I have met Palestinians, Acehnese, Rohingya, Uyghur, Hazara, Dinka, Zaghawa, Alawi, Baha'i, and other peoples. Some have been freedom fighters, others just fragile arthropods running for their lives on the rippling carpet we call 'Terra'. I have heard their stories.

'I'm so fed up with the hypocrisy,' I said. 'My Muslim friends have more integrity than most of my so called 'Christian' friends. And look what allegedly Christian nations have done to other peoples in the name of Jesus! That's not 'love'. It's sickening!'

I soon turned away from the church and ended up on a prodigal trajectory. My son was born under a Muslim identity in 2008.

When I returned to Oz in 2010 the label CALD (Culturally and Linguistically Diverse) had replaced the earlier term NESB (Non-English Speaking Background). Sadly, despite this development,

Australia's project of multiculturalism had flopped. We had left behind the assimilation policy for policies of toleration, appreciation, and celebration, respectively…only to reach the squalor of exploitation of identity in a 'free market' still reeking of colonial domination beneath the wrappings.

I took on volunteer work at a development network. Discovered that nothing had improved. It felt like reliving the 1980s all over again. Young peoples' stories revealed racially segregated playgrounds and experience of continued prejudice. Some of them found their feet and managed to assert themselves. A small few went off to join ISIS. The rest became submerged in the 'Millennial's' virtual underworld and rarely saw daylight.

Jesus came to me in an OBE (out of body experience) and told me I had got my study wrong. I had to reassess the situation, retrace my steps. Two years of study and the scales fell off. Paul had not been a Hellenist. Jesus had been crucified. But I didn't want to get burnt again. So I trod water for another four years. A difficult time without my son. Cut off due to the same cancerous religion that began in the world when Julia and I met. It wasn't until 2016 that the water became too stagnant to keep me alive.

I was in India. Living as a hypocrite between booze and Friday prayers. Broken. I fell on Jesus. I took a long walk, even up to the throne of Ayyappa. And then I realised how I had fallen out of the Vine. I longed to be back in the Body of Messiah again. And nothing else would satisfy.

It's 2018. Aunty says her son's dead. She's fighting for custody of her grandkids, who have seen things no human should ever have to see. I've had a child taken away from me too. We cry together.

Here I am back home – back in a church obsessed with the Author of Life. And I am loved. On the TV I see some 'comedy' where two Anglo men dress up as rural Arabs and speak like lobotomised monkeys inside a Bedouin tent, because apparently that is acceptable and funny again. I notice. So do my 'coloured' friends. We are saddened. The rest are oblivious. I utter a conciliatory whisper to an Aboriginal Jesus. He may be 'from above' but he also wears our red-blood flesh, just like Adam. Just like me.

A Sheep Called Jeffrey
Margot Ogilvie

'There's a sheep on the driveway.'

'Huh?'

My husband isn't really a morning person. I pack his lunch while he eats breakfast, usually in silence. He doesn't take too kindly to me being chatty and cheery so early in the day. But when I spotted a sheep strolling past the kitchen window, I thought I'd risk a comment.

'There's a sheep on the driveway,' I repeated.

'Must be one of Harry's broken through the fence,' he said without moving from the table.

Our neighbour sometimes had sheep on his property, but there were no others in sight. By the time my husband finished eating and left for work, the sheep was gone.

Or so I thought.

I got on with my day, one of those get-a-start-on-lots-of-jobs sort of days, looking out occasionally to see…you guessed it…the sheep wandering around our yard, calmly exploring new territory. Grazing. Content. Oblivious of his audience.

Two hours later, I was working at my computer, not even dressed yet, when I heard a banging at the front door. I looked up and saw a sheep standing on the front step looking through the glass door. Curious.

From a distance I noticed there were tags in his ear. He belonged to someone. Now if I could just get close enough to read them through the glass…alas, as soon as I approached, the sheep backed off, skittish.

I waited while he did a few laps of the house, now looking nervous. Agitated. Fearful. Lost. I'm not very rural, but I wondered if, when he'd settled down a bit, I might get close by cooing softly and approaching slowly with outstretched open hands. Like I'd seen them do with wild horses on all those movies. When the sheep nosed up to the glass door again, however, I chickened out on my courageous plan.

My son was home when the sheep 'knocked on the door' for a third time, nuzzling at the glass as if trying to get in. He named the sheep Jeffrey, though I favoured Scruffy, Baaarnabas or perhaps even Bo-Peep. Being of the technological generation, my son whipped out his phone to take a photo of the tags without having to get too close. Now why didn't I think of that? We zoomed in and easily read a name and phone number.

A young girl answered when I rang. Yes, her family owned sheep. They also lived on a property twenty minutes away, by car. Could Jeffrey have wandered that far? She didn't know if they were missing any animals. Her Dad wasn't home but she'd contact him.

Jeffrey continued head-butting my glass door and I hurriedly got dressed. I was still doing up buttons when Farmer Steve rang back, intrigued. Puzzled. Worried.

They agisted sheep on a property nearby. Jeffrey (not that he called him that, of course!) must have found a hole in the fence. As soon as he had Jeffrey back, he'd check the fences so no more would be lost. He'd be right over to collect him. With his dogs.

'How did you know it was mine?' Steve asked, after we'd discussed the situation at length.

'We read the tags,' I replied.

'We've lost a few sheep over the years and this is the first time anyone's ever phoned me. Makes those tags a good investment.'

He repeated his gratitude, apologised for any trouble and said he'd be here soon.

Sooner than I thought possible, an old farm ute sped up our driveway. Quite the commotion, with fenced trailer rattling, three dogs barking and tyres skidding on our gravel.

Enough to make a nervous sheep bolt. Which is just what Jeffrey did!

Steve said hello, thanking me again for ringing, apologising for the inconvenience, and explaining what he planned to do. This guy knew sheep. They're very sociable creatures, apparently. He told me Jeffrey no doubt spotted his reflection in the glass door and thought it was his flock. I'd have never thought of that.

He blocked Jeffrey's escape route with the vehicle and tried herding him in the right direction. Jeffrey took off the other way, down the bottom end of our property. Once the dogs were released, capturing Jeffrey seemed effortless. He didn't go without a fight, but with three dogs yapping at his heels, he had no choice but to hike up the ramp into the trailer.

With a wave my way from Steve, Jeffery was gone. Home where he belonged.

Leaving me with a brand-new image of God as the Good Shepherd. At first, I simply thought how great it was that Shepherd Steve had shown such enthusiasm for retrieving Jeffrey – how that reflects God's enthusiasm for saving the lost, with all of heaven celebrating as each one enters the fold.

I'd always assumed the Biblical parable was about non-believers – that Jesus was the Good Shepherd who went after the lost sheep (sinners) and brought them into the fold through salvation. Now that I'm saved, it had little to do with me!

But I realised with a jolt later that afternoon that I was wrong. Because Jeffrey had tags. He belonged to the shepherd. Yet he was no less lost. No less in need of rescue. Could it be that those of us who know salvation, who have the tag of the Holy Spirit marking us as his, can still sometimes wander from the fold and lose our way? The pressures and pull of life may leave us feeling nervous. Agitated. Fearful. Lost.

Not forever. No. Not eternally. Not 'unsaved' or de-tagged. Just not as close to the Shepherd as we could, should or used to be.

Once I'd started this fresh look at the 'shepherd parable', the similarities grew.

What did I learn from Jeffrey? Obviously, we don't need to tell God that one of his own has gone astray. He knows. But I learned to keep an eye out for lost sheep, so that I can relay their wandering to the Good Shepherd and participate in their retrieval. To keep my eyes and ears on the Good Shepherd so that I don't get lost myself. And that the Good Shepherd knows his sheep and will come quickly after us when we wander off, with all of heaven's resources at his disposal!

A Sheep Called Jeffrey

I'm so glad it was my place Jeffrey wandered into.

The Answered Prayer
Mikaela Tan Shyi Ern

In my school, we have activities every Friday. One of them is public speaking. Public speaking is one of my least favourite Friday activities. I have stage fright, meaning that I am scared to speak to a crowd. Every month, public speaking would come, each with a different topic. During public speaking, I would hide and stay out of sight so that I wouldn't be called. When I am called up, I start crying. I can't even stop crying throughout the whole presentation. This fear started four years ago in January 2015 when I first entered The Seed Resource Centre. My fear couldn't be conquered, but it did happen later in the year with the help of my friends.

Conquering my fear of public speaking was very hard. It happened on a fine October Friday in 2015. It was the last public speaking for the year. In my class, I was to go last in order to calm me down. My friend Joann was going before me. Apparently, she had stage fright too! So, we decided to present together. The next ten minutes was one of the most painful times of my life. It was so tough, without Joann holding my hand and God strengthening me, I might have burst into tears again. But thank God I am here to tell my story.

Finally, the grand moment arrived for me to go and speak. We walked up together very slowly. We decided beforehand that Joann would speak first, so she did. Her stage fright makes her speak very softly, more like she was mumbling. When she spoke, it was so soft that only I could hear her. I spoke out loud and clear with exact projection repeating what Joann was saying. Suddenly the hall fell in absolute silence. I was so confused; kind of like a person trying to figure out science formulas. In my head, I kept saying, 'Did I do that?' Quietly and calmly, the teacher checked with Joann to see if what I said was correct. Joann nodded and the class watched in silence and astonishment to see me conquering my fear. Then, it was my turn to present!

For the next five minutes, I presented my story, Goldilocks and the Three Bears. I was confident in everything and even added little

The Answered Prayer

actions that I didn't practice with my mom, such as reacting to porridge as Goldilocks tasted it. I also lay on the floor pretending to sleep in some parts. In the end, I was still crying, but this time, it was tears of joy and not fear. God had answered my prayer.

I found out later on that this happened because I thought of Joann's situation, and not my own. I wanted her presentation to go well, so I helped her without thinking much. God decided to help me because I put her presentation first. He helped me overcome my fear just so that I could help Joann. These two verses helped me to remember what God has done for me. 'Be strong and of a good courage, fear not, nor be afraid of them: for the Lord your God, he it is that goes with you,' and 'be not afraid of their faces: for I am with you to deliver you, says the Lord.'

There you have it, my first experience with God!

Heart Wide Open

Angela May

When my husband brought home a fat, blue-speckled puppy, I was not impressed. I distanced myself and left the loving up to him and our sixteen-year-old daughter. They called him Bender, after the tin man on their favourite cartoon show. Brittany adored the new puppy.

'Oh Dad, he is so cute.'

'Everyone, he is so cute. Come look,' she would say when someone visited.

I ignored his cuteness, as well as his puddles and spills on the polished wooden floors. I even ignored my daughter's infatuation until the puppy got sick. Very sick. He was barely in our care ten days when he became listless and had severe diarrhoea. Then I took notice.

My daughter was distraught. She had seen other pets die. This one was different though. This one involved God.

'Mum, why does God let our puppy suffer?'

I sucked in my sigh and felt my heart falter. This felt like a test, perhaps even a fight for my daughter's faith. Only a month before, she came home after a spiritual retreat for teenage girls, overflowing with faith conversations and a deep desire to share them with me. Her interest in church and anything Christian had been hanging by a thread before that weekend. In recent years, as a teenager she had become more interested in her outward appearance and partying with her friends. Now all of this recent joy and innocent faith appeared to be under fire. I was frightened.

'Mummy, why does God allow people and animals to die young?'

Oh dear. I could argue in my own head what I considered a reasonable theological answer. I even read widely on this question myself. But this was my daughter, and her heart was breaking. I scrambled for different words. Words that were comforting but also honouring of the deeper faith issues involved.

'Oh honey, let me tell you about this broken world we live in...' I began.

If I could have seen her heart, it would have been as wide open as her big brown eyes that peered back at me. She listened.

I was not satisfied. The puppy was not dead yet. And I believed in a God of hope and miracles. Her father delivered the sick puppy to the vet next morning. That day was Sunday. The little speckled body was poked and pricked and tubes were stuck down his neck and in his leg. He was given antibiotics, saline solution and myriad of other medications that did other things for his little body, to help him fight whatever dreadful virus he had succumbed to.

She leant on our breakfast bar. Perched on the wooden stool beside her I hesitatingly suggested, 'What do you think about us praying about this?'

'Sure, you do it though,' she said.

I shut my eyes. My prayer went something like this: 'Dear God. Little Bender is so sick. We really want you to heal him. If that is not your will, please take him quickly...' and with embarrassment I admitted, '...because we cannot afford the vet bill.'

Money was tight and the afterhours vet callout and specialist care was destined to be expensive. *Seriously, the puppy only cost $30!* I wanted to believe that God could and would heal our little puppy. I also knew we would not be the first people to see someone, or something die, after asking God for a miracle. *Maybe I am too careful. Maybe I have little faith.* The inner struggle went on. I did not want to be someone who claimed healing and then explain away the lack of answered prayer.

Brittany seemed satisfied with the prayer I uttered. I added a few more silent ones, alone and throughout the day. The past few years I prayed so hard and long for my daughter's renewal of her faith in God. I did not want something to come along and rob this openness to her faith in a living God.

Something did come along soon after this prayer. It was another dog, a little scruffy, white dog. He strayed into our backyard, looking hungry and accompanied by another brown dog. We captured this little one, concerned for his wellbeing. The brown one was wilier and ran off. Distracted for a while from Bender's problems, our family kept busy enquiring to find the little dog's owner.

Bender hung on for more treatment. He looked like rallying. One day clicked over into another day. We waited. My husband arranged for both of them to visit Bender at the vet's clinic. Brittany wept when she saw the little puppy, weak and listless in the newspapered cage. He hardly knew her. But she knew him. She loved him. She was hopeful.

Every morning the vet would call one of us to update us on the puppy's progress. I received his last call at work, announcing that overnight Bender had died. He would not be coming home.

The vet explained, 'Sorry, he did not have the strength to overcome.'

I let out a sigh. I didn't really want to make the call home. I knew I should deal with it before my working day got busy. Brittany's mobile rang five times before she answered.

'Bender's dead, Britt. I'm sorry… The vet just called.'

She broke down with a sob.

I wished I was there to hug her. I could only send a prayer. This did little to squelch the knot in my stomach. I pushed on to deal with my day.

When I arrived home that afternoon, I found my daughter lying on her bed. An invisible mantle of grief seemed to have settled on her sixteen-year-old shoulders. I lay down on her bed and she leant her head on mine.

'You've been busy?' I noticed. 'You've changed your bedding.'

She screwed up her face with a scowl. 'That scruffy little dog peed on my bed last night.'

As we already had a cranky old Maltese terrier that slept in the master bedroom, my daughter had begrudgingly scooped up the stray and enthusiastic pup, allowing him to sleep on her bed. She wished she had ignored him. As I had distanced my heart from Bender, she had distanced her heart for another reason.

'Mum, my heart hurts so much for loving Bender. I do not know if I ever want to open my heart again to love another dog.'

'Please, Britt, keep your heart open. I know it hurts to love.'

I wanted to reassure her that the God I knew would provide the comfort she needed. As her mother, I wished I could take the pain from her.

The vet disposed of our puppy for us. For some reason we did not collect his little body and bury it, like we had our previous dogs that were buried under the big tree in the front yard. He mailed us the invoice. For his services rendered and medications supplied, including a plasma infusion, ten days of care plus an emergency callout…a couple of hundred dollars. We were expecting a bill closer to six hundred dollars.

No one responded to our handwritten posters saying 'little dog found'. He was not microchipped nor registered with the council. No one came to claim this increasingly loving, white, scruffy little dog. He liked us. He even liked our old, cranky Maltese Terrier.

'Looks like this little puppy is going to stay here,' I announced to our daughter.

We were sitting together in our living room while both dogs were playing tug of war with my husband's work sock. Both pulling with equal force and growling.

She looked up. I looked at her. I realised then that perhaps the answer to my prayer was not the cheap vet bill but rather the gift of this little stray dog.

'We will have to name him', she declared.

'How about you name him?'

She thought awhile and with earnestness announced, 'I reckon Christmas. After all, it's Christmas time. Chrissy for short.'

A decade later, Chrissy lives up to his name. He reminds us regularly that he was God's gift to our family.

John Jenner
Olivia Harman

It is a puzzle to everyone and to myself why I have spent so much time looking for you, John Jenner! But here you are at last, or as it turns out, where you are supposed to be. That is in the pauper's corner of Cornelian Bay cemetery in Hobart, grave 254, compartment A. In fact, this grim section of the cemetery no longer exists as a separate entity. It did until 1998, when cemetery authorities relocated all paupers buried between 1872 and 1935 in one mass burial site. Now your bones all rest together, their location marked with a rather lacklustre plaque.

Today it is chilly standing here, but the Derwent estuary sparkles brightly in the background. The outlook is stupendous, unchanged since 1879, when the Cascades Invalid Depot buried you among other homeless derelicts. That was thirty years after you arrived on the *Mandarin* with 210 other convicts.

No, we are not related. Your existence was unknown to me until a year ago when my English uncle decided to ferret out information about our paternal ancestors from the Home Office. Your visitor today, the only one for a very long time, perhaps ever, is James Towner's great-great-great granddaughter. Remember him, your old partner in crime in the rural depths of East Sussex?

Claiming convict ancestry is quite fashionable nowadays but not, apparently, for my uptight relatives. They were hesitant to send copies of your criminal records to me in Australia. They worried it would be embarrassing. But eventually I got my hands on both your and my ancestor's documents, then tried to fill in the blanks from the Tasmanian convict archives.

The neat copperplate on your trial and transportation records is not easy to decipher. But what became clear is that, despite the fact both you and James Towner were respectively sentenced to fifteen and ten years transportation for sheep stealing in 1839, you were the only one actually shipped off to Tasmania. Did anyone tell you that after your trial, the rector of your parish petitioned the authorities claiming the harsh sentences were unjust? He, and other respectable members of your community, argued that your employer, an overseer of Poor Law work assignments, was a known crook, totally unfit for his responsible position. They provided proof that he had engineered your crime and that he was the one deserving punishment, not the two destitute farm labourers working under his orders.

Were you also aware that during your time in Lewes jail awaiting transportation, the rector kept up his efforts? He pleaded the fate of your wives, your five children and James's three once the two of you were sent away but all his efforts were in vain, at least on your behalf. Probably because you were older, aged 36, had already been in prison before for a short spell (forgive me, but your records report your character as 'bad' and 'very bad' during that prior incarceration), off you went. James Towner was only 30, of good character, so he obtained a reprieve, if one can call it that. His sentence was altered to serving his time on a hulk in Gosport doing hard labour in the port. The conditions in these prison ships was so bad that one in four prisoners died during their first year. With the rector continuing to plead his case, Towner was eventually pardoned in 1845 and reunited with his family. After another spell in jail later in life, he was buried in Barcombe graveyard among his relatives, aged 74. His daughter Phoebe married my ancestor Reuben Harman and their descendants managed to crawl up the social ladder after this little hiccup.

Considering these facts, why not drop you like a hot cake? It is not because my work as a historian brought me to Tasmania for a good ten years myself. My field is not convict history. Too grim, to depressing! Sorry to admit, it is not to try and work up your story as the romantic victim of an inhumane system either. True, convict records describe you as tall, dark-haired, and dark-eyed, so definite possibilities there but it is not about that, honestly. There is no moving historical novel in the planning.

So could it be strange feelings of connection because of my own enforced relocation to Australia 131 years after your own? I left under a dark cloud too, not from the law but from family problems. My beginnings in the Antipodes were challenging and lonely for a couple of years but compared to yours, it was a breeze. My time on this wild and beautiful island was great, in fact. So it has to be about more than that, surely.

Natural curiosity can be blamed, of course. In confidence, it is bewildering to me that several of my Tasmanian friends with genuine convict ancestors have no interest in them at all. Descendants still live close by in places where these convicts managed to make a life for themselves once freed. It would be so easy! When one watches: 'Who do you think you are?' or such similar programs, it is obvious many people would give an eye tooth to unearth tragic or shady pasts. The climax of their search usually ends with a big schmaltzy reunion with long lost relatives, lots of cups of tea and cathartic emoting.

But back to you, John Jenner. All that can be established is that once landed, the penal authorities assigned you to work gangs on the properties of two different free settlers. Seems you got into trouble for not sawing your quota of wood on one occasion. Your two-year probation period was extended for another term as punishment. Then at last, in 1847 or 48, a Ticket-of-Leave was granted and the freedom to work for wages in a set district. Unfortunately, your trail vanishes completely after this. Because ex-convicts were pariahs in the colony, it is likely you became an itinerant worker doing unskilled work until you were too old for it. This was the lot of many of your ex-mates, who finished up as beggars or back in jail, in lunatic asylums or charitable depots as you did. Living hells all of them: overcrowded, filthy, with harsh discipline and starvation diets. The superintendent of Cascades Depot recorded your status at the time of death, aged 77: *drifter, pauper, cause of death: senilis.*

So where do we go from here? None of your old pal Towner's descendants live in good old Barcombe anymore. My last remaining great-great aunt, another Phoebe, died there in the late 1950s. My grandparents took me to visit her a couple of times. She was ancient and sweet. Her little cottage was full of antiques, china, lace doylies and a stuffed fox in a glass case that fascinated me as a child. She seems to have done alright for herself, and so did her descendants.

However, it is fascinating that two different lots of Jenners can still be found in the Barcombe and Lewes phone directories. They could very well be your lot. Would they know anything about you or have you been conveniently forgotten? Contacting them is tempting just to find out. Tricky though! It would be great if they were pleased and interested. All could be kept low key. Just send them my research and maybe this little tin of earth collected from your burial site. Return you home to them if they wanted you back among the family. We will see... Divine will determined everyone's fate in this story. It was what it was. But it also has given me the opportunity to remember and honour your name. That's worth a try, no?

Jamie
Kaye Johnson

I sat down alongside Briony on the grassy embankment behind the javelin enclosure. Smiling back at us sitting there in the minimal shade on a hot, humid Darwin afternoon, her daughter Jamie picked up her javelin. Walking with her characteristic gait onto the running track, she stopped and launched the javelin into the air.

'Oh, that's a bit shallow,' Briony remarked, disappointed in Jamie's throw. 'She can do better than that,' she whispered to me, and with that Briony got up from the grass and went to meet Jamie to try to be coach for her girl.

Welcome to the world of amateur athletics, I thought. They'd travelled from one end of the country to the other for this competition; a mother and her athlete daughter. Jamie had received coaching for some time, but for this meet she was on her own with her mum. Briony encouraged her and Jamie made her second attempt, a little better, but off course. She'd achieved good distance this time, but it was a foul. Briony gave Jamie a double thumbs up, and Jamie grinned again at us.

I'd met the two of them the day before at the shot put medal ceremony. We were in Darwin as volunteer sports chaplains for the Arafura Games, and I decided to spend some time at the athletics arena, and watch the different sports there for the day. I'd noticed Jamie was in her South Australian representative gear, and wondered about her story. She was quite young, and had a definite limp as she walked away from the medal dais after receiving her silver medal.

When I caught up with her, she was excited to show me her medal and told me she came from Mt Gambier in southern South Australia and had come to Darwin with her mum to get more experience in competition at these games. She longed to go to the Olympic Games as a para-athlete, and this was just another step along the way to improve her skills.

'I'm competing again tomorrow morning in the javelin. Can you come and watch that too?' Not sure what our schedule was for the next day, I said I would do my best and she seemed delighted.

So there I was, moving with the shade, trying to find a comfortable spot, and to understand what was happening. I asked Briony how the medals were decided when there seemed to be athletes of varying standards and disabilities competing in the same event. She explained to me that they are classified according to their level of disability, and when they compete they are actually competing against the world record for their classification. So with the previous event Jamie had achieved a shot put 67% of the distance of the world record. However, another competitor in a different category had achieved at 72% of the world record for her category, and so won the gold medal, and Jamie the silver medal.

Jamie continued her event with another throw of the javelin, and this time it was a much better throw, soaring high in the air, and landing within the designated area point down and bouncing along the ground after it hit. She was jumping up and down in excitement, and turned with a huge grin on her face. That was the end of the preliminary rounds. Jamie had finished in first place and it meant she would be throwing last in the final three rounds to determine the medals.

I watched her in the medal rounds, trying to understand how someone with her physical limitations could throw a javelin that far. She had reduced ability in her run, especially her right side, and the power she could generate with the twist and thrust of her hips was quite amazing. But the overall power came from her strong upper body and toned arms. It made me realise just how hard she must have worked to gain the flexibility and strength she had. And, of course, she had loads of determination too, and a mum and family who totally supported her in her ambition.

She was a very excited young lady later in the day when she stood proudly in the gold medal position on the dais as we listened to 'Advance Australia Fair' being played with the Australian flag raised in her honour.

Briony had shared some of Jamie's story with me while we watched the javelin competition. She had been a passenger as a five year old in a car driven by Briony almost twenty years earlier. They were involved in a horrific accident not far from their South East home, and Jamie received devastating injuries, which left her right side paralysed, and considerable brain injuries which required emergency specialist treatment. She was airlifted to Adelaide by the Flying Doctor service that day and Briony was hospitalised in Mt Gambier with a fractured pelvis and broken arm.

When Jamie's condition deteriorated to the point they thought they were going to lose her, Briony was also airlifted to Adelaide so she could be with her daughter and her husband.

Miraculously Jamie survived, and the family have seen her overcome many obstacles in her recovery and rehabilitation. She had to learn to walk and talk again, and as the hard work continued, she developed a passion for athletics. So I found her at the Arafura Games, a 25-year-old young woman of passion and determination, supported by a devoted mum and a loving family back home.

Jamie had one more event to compete in the next day. It was the discus and she had been having difficulties with her technique in practice, Briony told me. For some reason the event was late starting, and Briony was on edge about it, because she had booked their flight home for 3 hours after the event was scheduled to begin.

When the event got under way, an hour late, we tried to find some shade in the burning conditions. There was no breeze at all, and the humidity made the conditions stifling. Briony watched the first couple of throws and expressed her frustration that Jamie wasn't throwing to the standard that she had set herself.

We watched as she trudged across the track towards us, and Briony again acted as her coach, encouraging her. The next throw was much better; she had relaxed. Again she had finished the preliminary round in good style and she was announced as the final competitor in the medal rounds.

By this time Briony was becoming anxious they would not catch their flight home. There was only 25 minutes left before they needed to leave the arena for the airport. She approached an official to explain their situation and he graciously allowed Jamie to move up the order to complete her three throws.

Briony jokingly said to me, 'If she wins a medal you can collect it for her! You're her number one supporter!' I laughed and responded, 'It's the only way I'll ever stand on a medal dais!'

So after hugs and exchanging contact details, they left to catch their plane. They had about twenty minutes to boarding time, and still had their hire car to return. Fortunately, the sports complex is very close to the airport, so we were confident they would make it. I promised to send photos of the medal presentation to them, and because the rest of the competitors still hadn't completed the final rounds we weren't sure if Jamie had won a medal.

I waited at the arena for the medal presentation; it was one of the last to be done that day. The official medal party made their way towards the dais and three Australian flags were being walked out by the flag bearers. There were only two competitors in the medal party, and I was starting to feel confident that Jamie had won a medal.

When the competitors stood behind the dais, they left a gap behind the gold medal step, and then the commentator named Jamie as the gold medal winner! I was so excited for her. I madly took photos and was able to send them to Briony. Within minutes I received a photo from Briony with Jamie photo-shopped into the frame standing on the gold medal dais! I didn't know then that they were well into their flight and Briony had been able to use the airline's wifi to send the picture back so quickly. I was so proud of this young girl and her amazing mum.

Yesterday, the twentieth anniversary of Jamie and Briony's accident, I read the details of the crash from a Facebook post by Briony. It contained the newspaper clipping from twenty years ago of Briony's story; the horror of the accident, the fear for her daughter's life, and the wonderful service given by the Royal Flying Doctor Service in their retrieval and transfer of Jamie to the medical services she needed. Without them, Jamie would not have survived.

No Place like Home

Gaynor Faulkner

That beauty case was the best present I'd ever received. It was the quintessential gift choice for a grown up, sophisticated seven-year-old like me. A perfect accessory for a kid who loved to promenade in her mother's old ball gowns and pirouette around the lounge room with a pink satin lampshade wedged around her waist like a ballerina. And it wasn't even my birthday!

Mum presented the parcel to me one seemingly normal Sunday morning, just before church. The beauty case looked just like Samantha's in *Bewitched*. Its interior was a bridal veil – a confectionary of fluffy white tulle and satin. Potion bottles sat in shirred pockets like elegant swans. I couldn't wait to fill their bellies with a rainbow of scented concoctions.

My oldest sister was a bit of a tomboy and wasn't particularly fussed about my new acquisition but Kathy, my youngest sister was livid. 'Hey, how come *she* gets to have a beauty case – where's mine?' she demanded pointing an accusing finger at me. I smugly jumped on the bed, swinging the coveted beauty case back and forth, back and forth.

'Never you mind now!' snapped Mum. I glanced at her in surprise. I was usually the one in trouble. This day couldn't get any better – and Mum hadn't even told me off yet for jumping on the bed. Then in a stage whisper she said to Kathy, 'Your sister is a very brave young lady indeed! She's going to go away for a little while to get her tummy fixed in hospital.' Mum's voice broke a little then and softened. 'She'll need that beauty case to put all her special little things in.'

Brave? For a wonderful moment I basked in Mum's praise like a cat stretching in the sun. And then my jumping came to an abrupt end. *Hospital*? That was news to me. *No! I'm not going to hospital – I'm not even sick!* I almost protested. But then I looked down at my sophisticated little beauty case, still dangling on my arm like a handbag draped on a movie star and began to think that hospital didn't sound too bad after all.

Straight after church I was duly deposited in hospital. Mum, Dad and my sisters stayed for a while before the visitor bell indicated it was time to go. It scared me that Kathy no longer looked at me in envy, indeed she looked like she might cry. I sat up proudly in the big hospital bed and hugging my prized little beauty case, I tried not to cry myself.

The nurses and Matron seemed terrifying to me. They spoke with icy authority and always seemed in such a hurry. Hospital in those days didn't allow parents to stay overnight and visiting hours were limited and strictly adhered to. I was placed in a room with two beds. An ancient old lady presided in the other bed. Her snow-white hair blended in so well with the crisp white bedlinen that it was quite some time before I even discovered her.

That night the old lady's snoring sounded like a terrifying monster – the sort that could very well snatch treasures from a beauty case. Like a lump of ice, the case felt cold and hard as I clutched it closer to me while I tried to sleep.

Painfully waking up after my operation the next day, I discovered that the stitches in my stomach prevented me from walking. It wasn't good news for a kid as hyperactive as me. The aftereffects of the ether made my head go around and around and around until I was sick.

'Nurse!' hollered a gravelly authoritative voice. It was the old lady and she was pressing her buzzer like a crazy person. 'The little girl's been ill. You'll need to clean her up immediately,' she barked – although there was nobody yet in the room.

As I waited for a nurse, I gazed out the window at the orchard across the road. The trees glowed with fiery orbs of fruit. Their leaves quivered in the wind like party jelly. Those trees looked so free – like they were having fun. It made me think longingly of our own fruit block and how very much I wanted to be there right then.

'I'm Mrs Blake,' the old lady suddenly announced after I had been attended to. 'Hospitals can be very scary places at times, can't they, dear?' Her eyes were the same colour as my aqua crayon. Drawing me in. I nodded shyly.

Later that afternoon I had to go to the toilet. I pressed my buzzer. Nobody came so I pressed it again and then again. Suddenly, it was too late. I was mortified!

Eventually, an obviously harassed nurse bustled into the room. She shook her head at me and then clicked her tongue with impatience.

'You should be ashamed of yourself. It's absolutely disgusting!' Mrs Blake spat from the other bed. I hung my head in abject humiliation.

'That poor little girl has been buzzing her bell for ages for someone to bring in the bedpan and you've jolly well caused an accident being so slow about it!'

I looked over at Mrs Blake and grinned. That was the moment I realised she was going to be my friend.

In accordance with hospital rules, my family could only visit me for one hour every afternoon. The time seemed interminable between visiting hours but my new friend helped immensely to assuage my loneliness. The nurses now called us chatterboxes. I never found out exactly what was wrong with her except she couldn't walk either. And she was very, very old – so ancient that even Nan called her Mrs Blake.

In the afternoons Mrs Blake continued to have her naps but I no longer thought her snoring sounded like a scary monster. It sounded more like the snuffle of newborn puppies or raspberries blown on a baby's belly – and for some reason now it soothed me.

One day I awoke to a different sound. I peered over at Mrs Blake and was horrified to see that she was crying. Concerned, I enquired if she was all right.

'Yes, thank you, my dear,' she told me dabbing at her tears. 'I'm just missing my two dear boys that are gone now.'

That confused me. Mrs Blake had spoken at length about her family but she hadn't spoken about any missing boys.

'One was very brave and died fighting for us in World War II – a long, long time ago. The other was working hard in the quarry when a terrible explosion happened.' Mrs Blake's voice trembled as she reminisced. I could tell that she was trying really hard not to cry. I could feel my own warm tears trickle down my cheeks.

'Good gracious, don't you cry too, dear,' Mrs Blake told me with a start. 'I'm only sad because I miss them so much. *I'm* the one that's away from home. They're so safe and happy now.' She smiled widely. 'I'm only crying for me – just selfish. I want to see them and give them a great big hug.'

She nodded at me slowly then and with a wistful expression said, 'That will only happen when it's my time to go too. Oh, I so look forward to seeing my beautiful boys again. Heaven is a place just full to the brim with love and happiness.' She grabbed her tissue box and waved it in the air joyfully as if she were young again. 'And not...a...single...tear there – unlike here!' she added, laughing.

As Mrs Blake spoke about heaven and her boys I remember the fading sun seemed to paint everything pink and gold in that stark hospital room. Mrs Blake herself appeared to radiate light. I thought she looked just like an angel. I had never heard anyone say that they'd like to be in heaven before. I'd always imagined it as a faraway and gloomy place but Mrs Blake had made it sound so magical and fun – like Disneyland.

At the end of that week my family came to collect me from hospital. It's funny; I was so busy saying my goodbyes to Mrs Blake that I almost forgot my little beauty case. Matron had to actually scurry after me in the corridor to return it.

I remembered Mrs Blake's beautiful faith in heaven a few years later when my grandfather died. And I recalled it a few days ago when a small child confided in me how sad they were about losing their father.

I insisted on visiting my friend from time to time over the next couple of years until she died. When Mum told me the sad news after school that day, I blinked away my tears. I could almost see Mrs Blake's joyful smile. I knew that she was exactly where she wanted to be. She was embracing those sons she was so proud of – in that wonderful place she'd called home.

I Raise a Hallelujah

Yasmin Esther

My mother slid the toggle button to accept the call from my grandma. Her face turned pale and she said, 'I'll be right there,' in a shaky voice. We got into the car, and Mum was praying in tongues and driving at the speed limit. Our grandparents had met with an accident at a busy intersection between our school and another, while attempting to go and pick up their glasses from the optometrist. We parked somewhere close to the accident and ran over. The second I saw the wreck, I burst into tears. The why, what and how mixed in my mind.

I raise a hallelujah, in the presence of my enemies [1]

It was pretty bad. My grandfather had dozed off when driving and had hit the pole on the median strip. The car had flipped and was now balanced dangerously on the roof. The airbags had failed to go off. The first thing I saw other than the car was an emergency services crew who were pulling Grandad out and working with the paramedics to get him onto a stretcher. Amazingly, he was conscious, even laughing, as he entered the ambulance! Police were questioning bystanders, and one reassured us that they were fine.

I raise a hallelujah, louder than unbelief

My grandmother had also entered another ambulance and was praying as the paramedics lifted her to get on the stretcher. She had a gash through one hand, but looked totally fine except for a few cuts. Later she confided in me that all she remembered was getting out of the car through the window, which should have been physically impossible. But we both believe there was an angel guarding them that day.

---

1 Song lyrics copyright Bethel Music 2018.

I raise a hallelujah, my weapon is a melody

Grandma wanted someone to accompany her in the ambulance, so I hopped in. I recall Olly, the driver, wondering why we were both so calm. Grandma was witnessing to the nurse. He was listening to her. The ambos said to Grandma, 'You must have someone up there looking after you.' We got to the Prince Alfred hospital, renowned for its first class trauma care, in half the time it usually takes. 'It's my guardian angel,' Grandma explained, beaming. 'Jesus, thank you for this small blessing!' I praised God in my head.

I raise a hallelujah, Heaven comes to fight for me

Grandma was discharged that night with only a broken rib. God of the impossible! Unfortunately, Grandad wasn't quite as lucky. Due to previous health issues, his condition deteriorated quite a bit. He was taken to the Coronary Care Unit. I remember visiting and him not being able to talk, hooked up to lots of machines and an oxygen mask. I heard whispered conversations about Intensive Care. Brain bleeds. Coronary angioplasty. He barely shifted in the hospital gown. I cried and hugged my Mum afterwards. 'Why?' It didn't make sense. They had served God as pastors for thirty years previously.

I'm gonna sing, in the middle of the storm

The next time I saw him was on the Monday. He was off the breathing machine, talking, joking and was praying for a nurse. His brain bleed had 'disappeared'! He definitely did not look like he had two days prior, when he had been fighting for his life with millions of wires sticking out of him! There was even a little talk of discharge and hospital transfer. He grinned at me when I handed him a copy of the latest *Stories of Life*, promising to read it in his spare time.

Louder and louder, you're gonna hear my praises roar

Just when it seemed like things were getting better, that we were slowly climbing up the mountain again, another challenge came our way. My mum, who had had a heart procedure a few months earlier, started experiencing symptoms again. Unfortunately, her stent had collapsed and her heart was again 99% blocked. She had angioplasty on the same day as Grandad. I was scared now – everyone at church had put responsibility on me, and they were saying things like, 'So, you're taking care of your siblings, and doing all the chores, and looking after Grandma, Grandad and Mum, etc?' I always just smiled and tried to nod, although I felt guilty for not helping as much as I supposedly was. I just went to bed and listened to my aunt and her then fiancé. I fell down the mountain again. But I trusted in God, and slowly rebuilt my faith on his rock-solid word.

Up from the ashes, hope will arise.

My grandfather needs dialysis, and help with other things as well, but by the grace of God, my grandmother has looked after him and they do not need a carer. I believe God is a miracle worker – Grandad is living proof.

Death is defeated, the king is alive!

The Golden Detour
Kaitlin Turland

'Take off the gold earrings of your wives, sons and daughters!' the man yelled to the people. 'This God who brought us out of Egypt has obviously forsaken us. Let us take matters into our own hands: make a god for ourselves; let us bow down to what we can see. Then we will get to the Promised Land sooner: Moses doesn't care about us and will prolong the journey uselessly!'

Thousands of years later, I stared at a long, steep track meandering into the distance: the snake path with many detours. We had tackled Mount Sinai just a few days prior and were now grasping for the prize of Mount Catherine, just a few kilometres away. Our trail mix and 'medicine', a large packet of coloured snakes, coated our teeth with sweetness. We frequently rested on sandy brown boulders, lest we grew weary and our ambition melt into grumbles of lassitude. The smell of dust was in the air, the breeze on our faces, my far-from-ostentatious but favourite pair of sneakers crunching the gravel beneath my feet. We examined with interest the flat-topped stones with the markings of ancient roots. It was a labyrinth of thin black scars branching out to hundreds of dead ends, with only one that reached the other side.

Our guide, a Bedouin man, wore a faded cream-coloured long galabeya and a checked keffiyeh, rather similar to the garb we wore as shepherds in our church's Christmas pageant. He and Dad were a few steps ahead of us, their conversation exploring other tourist sites in the area. My focus was the rugged rocky summit; the path was hidden from view as the mountain dared me to conquer it. As I gazed at the track behind me it screamed affirmation of the progress I had made, then I peeked at the peak ahead of me to measure my current strength against the journey ahead.

The route we would evidently take slowly moulded into shape in my mind's eye and I could see it as clearly as a large print book. It gradually trailed behind us and we reached the shoulder of the mountain, where I knew we would turn left to mount the final leg of the journey to the summit.

But we did not. The guide led us on a detour.

He led us *down*.

Aware that my perseverance was hanging by a single thread, my anger raged like heat from a furnace. How dare he waste the motivation we had because we were nearly there, by extending the path so we were not? I was certain he was out to get us, sure that he just wanted us to walk unnecessarily further…

My futile complaints led to nothing but a dead end of frustration, bubbling in the cauldron of my voice. If the guide was not going to lead us the *right* way then I would diverge from the track and get to the top myself. Much quicker than I would with them. I turned around and did just that, the rocky slope off the track calling my name in a low, melancholy drone, gleaming in lustrous allure. My parents yelled my name in a much louder, more alarmed tone.

'Follow the guide, he's the expert!'

'Get back here; you're going the wrong way!'

My determination to defy the guide who had antagonised me fired me up the mountain, the opposite direction to the rest of the group. My slow weary trudge had become an impassioned strut as I dodged the rocks around my feet to reach my goal.

Then the hot cloud of anger that hung over my mind began to lift and the fog that had blurred the senselessness of my actions melted away into a clear solid picture. Who was I to think I knew better? The guide was here to lead us to the summit and I had gone the wrong way.

I reluctantly reunited with my family on the guide's route. It was roundabout and much longer than I had anticipated, but we reached the summit in the end. We later found out that the route I had mapped out in my head led to unscaleable cliffs and a military base.

This light and momentary journey brought me to a highway of realisation that far outweighed it all; a lesson that was more precious than all the gold in the world. Despite the less severe consequences, my episode of obstinacy was not dissimilar to the event that occurred nearby thousands of years prior. Like the Israelites, my impatient lack of trust caused me to irrationally turn

The Golden Detour

my own way, pursuing the gold-plated road I could see rather than trusting the guide to lead us to the destination laden with diamonds. For *in their hearts humans plan their course, but the Lord establishes their steps* (Proverbs 16:9 NIV).

Who are we to challenge his guidance?

God My Confidence
Ivan Yap

There's a scar on my forehead. While it reminds me about how I 'truly' became a Christian, it's also a memorable thing that happened to me two years ago.

In 2017, when I was 13, my school held a marathon in a park. My friends and I didn't get any placing because we were not running, we were just enjoying the view of the park. When it ended, my two friends and I started walking back to my home.

As we were passing by a lake, my friend Deric and I started throwing some huge stones into the lake. My friend Darren was trying to stop us but we ignored him. When I squatted down beside my friends, trying to pick up a larger stone, Daric accidentally hit me with a stone. I was terrified when blood trickled down my face.

Luckily, there was a security guard who saw what happened. He quickly took a cloth to cover my wound. Then he brought me to a shelter. He asked for my parent's number and he informed them what had happened. When they arrived, my parents thanked the security guard and rushed me to the hospital.

My parents prayed for me when I was having my surgery. During the surgery, I felt calm and did not feel fear, because I knew that God was with me.

After the incident, I started to desire to know more about God, because when I was younger, I used to call myself a 'Christian' without knowing exactly who God was. I read the Bible carelessly before the miraculous event took place. But after this, I began reading the Bible with my heart. Also, I used to hate studying a lot before, because it was hard for me, but after I encountered God I felt different about studying.

After the incident, I felt that my relationship with God was so close that I could feel him even in hard times. I really thank God for letting this scar be on my head, because it reminds me that God is with me no matter what.

Three Seconds, Bus Stops and Log Trucks

Megan Higginson

I gripped the steering wheel as another log truck rushed by on its way to the paper mill. My car rocked from side to side. Everything felt surreal. There was no way I was here, on the side of the road at this bus stop in another town with just my daughter. There was no way I would say goodbye to her as she got on a different bus to the same school and I go back to a strange house.

And yet it was all very real. The rocking of the car said it was real. The silence of my daughter said it was real. The warm breeze blowing through my open window said it was real. I was one of those women who had left her husband.

'Do you think God still loves us, Mum?' Ashlyn asked.

I took a deep shuddering breath. 'I'm sure he does, honey.' I placed my hand on hers. 'He wouldn't have made a way for us to leave when we had to if he didn't care about us and love us.' And then the verse we needed came to mind.

I smiled and reminded her. 'For I am convinced that neither death nor life, neither angels nor demons, neither the present nor the future, nor any powers, neither height nor depth, nor anything else in all creation…will be able to separate us from the love of God that is in Christ Jesus our Lord,' we finished together.

Ashlyn gave a weak smile. 'I thought so. It's just what someone said to me at school. But no one really likes them anyway. They're mean.'

Move, came a whisper.

Move? Whatever for? I've parked my car in this exact spot every single day for nearly two weeks.

Move, came the prompting again.

I don't understand, God. Why?

Move now. The prompting was insistent.

I shrugged. *Okay, God. It won't hurt me to move the car.* I started up the car and moved further off the road. Ashlyn looked at me with a query in her eye and opened her mouth to speak as I parked the car and switched off the engine. She never got the chance.

A roar of yet another log truck screamed up behind us. We glanced around just as the truck swerved off the road and into the space we had just vacated seconds before. Our mouths dropped open as we watched the driver fight the truck back onto the road and drive on to his destination, never knowing he had been seconds away from wiping us out.

But we knew. We knew we had just been there, in that very spot. I felt a buzzing in my head. Everything still felt surreal, like I was walking through a dream. And that question, 'Does God still love us?' That question was answered loudly with a resounding, 'Yes!'

In a Manger
Joanne Prenzler Smith

Our son was born in November. A long-awaited second child I thought I might never have.

Christmas was fast approaching when our pastor asked if we would let our son be baby Jesus in the Christmas Eve production. Our church, like many others, loved to tell the Christmas story with the children dressed as Mary and Joseph, angels, shepherds and wise men. I was a bit nervous about leaving our baby in the care of children, but when it was decided that I would sit among the little ones we agreed. We had a doll on hand to swap over if he became unsettled.

Christmas Eve arrived and I made sure our son was well fed and freshly changed just prior to the service. As people took their seats I placed him in the wooden manger at the front of the church and stepped away. Despite all that was going on around him, our son, wrapped in a white cloth and nestled in his little bed, promptly fell asleep.

I know we would have sung carols such as 'Silent Night,' 'O Little Town of Bethlehem', 'We three Kings of Orient Are'. I don't remember exactly how the performance went that night. The story unfolded of the Virgin Mary called to carry a child that was God's and not her new husband's. Of the young husband shocked but standing by his wife after an angel visited him. Of them travelling the rough road to Bethlehem where Jesus, the Saviour of the World, was born and was worshipped by men of both high and low rank. How angels sang to welcome him to earth.

The details are a bit of a blur. But I know how closely I watched my son just out of reach and in the care of others. This child was my miracle, my gift from God, and here I was entrusting him to children. Did God feel this way about his child?

Our son had lain quietly throughout the service, sleeping peacefully in his makeshift bed. We got to the part of the story where God came to earth, as Jesus, became a human baby for us. Our son stirred and stretched, waving one little arm high in the air.

An audible gasp ran through the congregation as they suddenly realised the baby in the manger was real. It brought home that Jesus' birth is not just a nice story, it actually happened. He was and is real. A gift, a person and a promise.

When the service finished I was able to take my son and hold him. He slept through the whole thing, oblivious to what was going on around him. But he played a role that Christmas by simply lying in a manger.

A Thousand Dollars

Rusty A Lang

'And my God will supply all your needs according to His riches in glory in Christ Jesus' (Philippians 4:19 NASB).

Another thousand dollars was needed.

A month's overseas ministry in East Africa was booked. The budget was already stretching my bank account and faith. Then an unexpected additional expense connected with the trip loomed in front of me.

Since I am not in the business of printing money I decided to let God handle this. Strange as it may seem, I was not at all concerned. I had seen God come through many times when something is his idea and I knew this trip was planned by him.

A few days after I had given the need over to God, a knock came on the door.

I was quite ill that day so my husband answered it. A lady handed him a card in an envelope and left. When I opened it, twenty fifty dollar bills fell out. As I counted them through the tears flowing freely, my praise went up to God. It was exactly one thousand dollars.

No one except my husband, myself and God knew about this need.

Unbeknownst to me, a young married couple in our small country fellowship had been told by the Holy Spirit many months before to put aside a thousand dollars as God would have a need for it.

As the months passed they continued to pray over every need they heard of, but God would not release the finance. Then when they heard about my upcoming trip, both the husband and wife knew it was to be given to me. God had it in hand long before I received the invitation to minister; long before I knew of the extra expense.

That is the God who is pleased to bless us when we are in his will.

Only God Knows
Priscilla Ng

It was a chilly Thursday morning and my school was currently in a convention that started on the 28th of August, 2017. The convention was held in Kota Kinabalu, Sabah, in an ACE, an Accelerated Christian Education school. It was my very first convention and I was so nervous for this day because it was the day when my school would perform our GBS − Group Bible Speaking. This was our sixth year participating in this event and I was part of it. We have always won ever since we entered. However, on that day something happened that my team did not expect and it was the most heartbreaking and faith-shaking thing that happened.

The day went something like this: It was around 6 in the morning. The sun had not yet risen on the horizon, but the birds were already working at this time and so was my school. I woke up especially early on that day and was able to get a good spot within the toilets before the other girls and began my short routine. About an hour later, the girl's group gathered together and we started our morning devotion and a little prayer for God to bless the day. In the prayer, I believe there was a mention of how God should let his will be done that day and if there were any troubles that day, we should not lose hope.

It was currently 9 in the morning, but GBS registration was at 10. However, time passed quickly and it was soon time for the registration. My team gathered by the front of the main hall where the event was to be held. We waited for our coach to brief us and give us a few words of encouragement. As it was time for us to head in, the judges called all of us over for a short prayer of blessing and courage as they did for other teams before us. Then it began. The annoncer started us off and we all took our starting positions. Even though we had many acrobatics, a part where our timings were off for a stomp, and a little lagged in our speech in some parts, we pushed through to the end and we finished on a high note.

At the end of the day, as we were preparing for our night rally, we were expecting a call from the judges for our GBS. The reason is that the call was for a command performance, which meant that our school had the most suitable and best choreography that could be shown. However, we never received that call and that worried us as well as the supervisors. In the midst of our panic, one of our sponsors came in and called for the GBS team.

We gathered into one corner of the room and she started her announcement with an apology. Apparently, she had given the judges the wrong sets of papers and so the performance we did could not be checked. This crushed the GBS team's spirit when we arrived in the main hall and the team which was called for the command performance came up. I and a few of the other team members broke into tears of sorrow and disappointment, Some of our supervisors were praying and weeping for us as well.

When the awards came, our GBS team got up and raised our heads high because I believe at that moment, the Spirit was in us all telling us to not grieve and not to fear for he has seen what we've done. So as the other GBS teams lined up to receive the awards we stood tall and somewhat composed. And they started to announce the winners, 'Coming in the sixth place is …'

Then the fifth, fourth, then third! At this point the little beats of my heart could be heard in my ears, I was silently praying for God to give me faith and courage. Then the announcers paused at the second place,

'And the first place goes to The Seed Resource Centre!'

Just that one sentence brought joy to my heart. We didn't break the winning streak. We were The Seed Resource Centre and we had just witnessed the mercy and faithfulness of God and, just like our choreography, we burst out into tears of joy, we hopped, cheered, and praised God for his mercy upon us. Only God knows what happened that day, but I'm glad and thankful and God has shown us his mercy as a few of us, including me, were strengthened and changed by this event.

My Journey Climbing Mount Kinabalu

Leanne Low

June 2013 was one of the most exciting months of my life. I was about to embark on an adventure that not many people get the opportunity to have in their lifetime, but I had the privilege of experiencing it at a young age. That was climbing the highest mountain in Malaysia - Mount Kinabalu.

The journey started at the beginning of 2013 when we met a family friend. He had climbed Mount Kinabalu over 60 times and he taught us some techniques for mountain climbing. From there, our group gathered every week to prepare by hiking some hills. Our group comprised of five families. I was one of the youngest in the group, so I struggled a lot at the start, but with the motivation from my friends and family, I soon got used to the intensity of our weekly trainings.

As the date for the start of the climb was nearing, more preparations on top of our usual training had to be made. Firstly, my father had to make bookings for our flights, accommodation, and much more. Another important thing we had to pay much attention to was the temperature. As we climbed to higher altitudes, the temperature would gradually decrease and the air would become thinner, so getting proper clothing and decent sized luggage bags to fit our clothes while travelling was crucial. Food was also something else that we needed a lot of in order to have enough energy to sustain us. My mother packed a load of snack bars and chocolates, and I ate almost all of them! My favourite part throughout the whole process of preparation was my family's countdown chart. A large calendar was stuck on the wall of our home which marked the milestones of the whole journey. My mother also pasted motivational quotes and important things to remember on the calendar. We would then cross out each day with a big 'X'. Each time we did that, the more anxious we felt leading up to the actual day.

After weeks of preparation, the day finally arrived. Everyone was pumped and excited. We arrived at Kinabalu Park and stayed at a nearby hotel for a night. In the morning we awoke, packed our bags, and made our way to Timpohon Gate, which was the 'starting line' of the climb. Throughout the entire journey, there were rest stops for climbers to stop to catch a breath and eat some food such as the chocolate we packed. Each family was provided with a guide to lead and help us explore the mountain better. Our friend we met at the start of the year also climbed the mountain with us and he even brought his ukulele along. He lightened everyone's spirits by singing songs and dancing along the way. We also learned a traditional Mount Kinabalu song from the native guides.

As expected, the temperatures were cold and got worse as we climbed higher. It was tough, as the path was steep and the cold temperature made us uncomfortable. Since there were other children on this climb, the plan was to take it slow and finish the whole journey in three days rather than the usual two. The first day was slow moving but at last we reached one of the main stops, which was Laban Rata. Here, we could lodge for a night and continue on the next day to the peak. We thought we could relax there but things weren't as comfortable as we thought. The showers, for example, only had freezing cold water so some of us didn't even shower. Nevertheless, we were grateful for a place to stay and made the most of our time there.

Day two was the day that everyone was most amped about. It was when we would be hiking to the peak! Each of the kids had a personal guide as this portion was going to be the most rocky part of the entire hike. There was also a rope provided for us to hold on to for extra grip. So off we went early in the morning, making our way to our ultimate goal: the peak. The feeling from the day before still carried on and the cold temperatures still bothered us, but we didn't give up. Our perseverance was rewarded by the view that awaited us at the peak. It was truly splendid, glorious and breathtaking. It made us feel we had accomplished something. We were able to enjoy God's wonderful creation before us like never before and it was just so perfect. Of course, besides enjoying the view, we took plenty of photos to remember this moment. We couldn't stay as long as we liked as the wind was strong, making the weather cold. Furthermore, we were eager to climb back down to Laban Rata to get some rest. We stayed there another night and on the next day we hiked all the way back down to Timpohon Gate.

At the end of our trip, I received my certificate of completion. I felt so proud of myself for what had been accomplished and so thankful for this experience. The whole trip could not have been finished without the motivation of my family and friends, but above all, without my Heavenly Father's help.

A Good Friend
Jemuel Wong

As I entered the school hall, a roaring wave of voices assaulted me. A few students cast curious glances my way, because I was new to the school. Most of them just ignored me and continued talking with their friends. Very soon, the teachers called the students, including me, back into our respective classrooms.

Inside the classroom, the teacher introduced me to the rest of the class. I waved at them and tried to smile, nervous as I was. Some smiled back, clearly pleased to have a new potential friend; most, however, just continued staring at me, sceptical of my intentions. I got seated in my chair, wishing that the clock would go faster.

I wasn't quite the socialising type. My background as a home-schooled child meant that I had never really had the chance to make good friends. The only companions I had were my siblings, two younger brothers and two younger sisters. I was quite close to both my parents and my siblings, and loved them deeply. I was content and happy.

Unfortunately, in the year that I turned 15, I was forced to leave my family to study abroad. I was admitted to the school and lived with the school principal, Ms Fiu See. Life was dull and I found no pleasure in school or at 'home'. Some students in school then began to pick on me, seeing that no one would come to my aid.

Gradually, my resentment towards those who bullied me made me cold-hearted. I resisted those who tried to breach my wall of isolation, and ignored those who wanted to befriend me. I successfully deflected any attempts to make friends with me. That is, until Grace came.

I met Grace, Ms Fiu See's daughter, in the house one day after school. I was exhausted and wanted to be alone. But Grace greeted me with a big smile and introduced herself. She had just returned from studying in Australia to visit her family.

I originally did not want to talk to Grace and avoided her questions. But she was persistent and eventually I gave in. We started chatting with some small conversation and got to know more about one another.

Soon we became good friends and did many fun things together. Once we even baked a cake for her family! Grace also taught me how to make new friends and introduced me to many of hers. Before long, the walls I built around my heart came tumbling down and I made a few new friends very quickly.

But after some time she had to return to Australia. I was quite sad to hear this, so I prayed to God. As I prayed, I realised that God had put the right people at the right place just at the right time. Even more, God had been with me the whole time! From my most depressing times to my happiest moments, God was by my side. Truly, God is the best friend one could ever have.

A Lesson for Life
Alan Blunt

We were lucky kids. There was never much money, yet we seven siblings always ate healthily, and were loved and comfortably housed and clothed. The only grandparent I knew was kindly Mary Cooney. She told stories of folklore she had learnt from her Irish parents, of mischievous 'little people', and the awesome power of the devil.

Grandma never said a hostile word about anyone, even the despotic cruelty of Ireland's English occupiers, or Martin Luther. She explained that although Luther had caused the great split in Catholic Christianity, God alone was his judge.

During Mary's early life anti-Jewish slogans, and signs declaring *No Catholics Need Apply,* or *Aboriginals Keep Out*, freely spelled out religious bigotry and racial discrimination. However, remnants of bigotry surfaced when my older sister and I attended a tiny Darling Downs school in 1948.

The first morning break we were accosted by a family of two boys and a girl. The leader, an older, bigger boy of fifteen, announced that Catholics were unwanted outsiders. Patty explained that the Catholic Church was the only true religion, but God would reward all good people. The bully shoved her over. I started swinging punches and was quickly punched down. We retreated while the other kids looked on silently. I knew I'd get no sympathy from Dad for telling tales, and Patty said she wouldn't worry Mum.

Perhaps I spoke out of turn before the bully flattened me the next day. Patty led the way to the teacher. 'There are two sides to every argument,' he explained. 'Nevertheless, I'll speak to them.'

'Unfair,' Patty protested. She was sternly told not to give cheek.

The following day we retreated to a far corner of the playground. Most of the kids tagged along. The bully ordered us to 'Keep moving,' and I put my fists up.

'Don't Alan,' Patty cried.

'Stop,' a boy shouted. The bully advanced on him, but he didn't flinch. His little sister stood by his side, and their attitude emanated certainty and courage:

'We are Lutherans,' he declared. 'My father said we are not to stand idly by while you bully the Catholics.' He emphasised his speech with biblical quotations, and his words carried the power of the pulpit although they were spoken by a young boy in the shade of whispering gum trees. Whipped with words, the bully walked away. Seventy years later that vision of religious courage banishing bigotry still inspires me.

Over the next couple of weeks the brother and sister sat with us. We joined in skipping and playground games and, being kids, soon found growing familiarity promoted friendship, and that going to different churches on Sundays made little difference to our human needs and desires at play.

A Certain Stranger
Kylie Gardiner

The sun was low on the horizon as I drove. I pulled down the visor but the glare was still biting. I flicked down the sunglasses perched on my head but I still couldn't see the road in front of me. Then I felt the wheels mount the kerb. For a split second I saw the pole out wide before it ripped straight through the engine. It was centimetres from me, crushing the bonnet and sending my heart through my mouth. Adrenaline was running. I was in shock. I felt wobbly and clammy. My hands still grasping the wheel. I looked at the pole next to me. I sat there for a few moments and talked to myself. I was alive. No one else was hurt. Gingerly, I got out of the mess of twisted grey and blue metal. I stood and looked at my car while traffic whizzed by on the six lane highway. This was pre mobile phones. There were no telephone booths in sight. I sent up a silent prayer. Lord help! I have no idea where I am. I felt helpless.

Then I saw him, crossing the busy highway. What kind of crazy thing was that? The man zig zagged across three lanes and reached the median strip and I realised he was heading for me. Nimbly dodging traffic he was stopping for no one. As I watched him getting closer I suddenly felt fearful. Who was he? Was I safe?

Then he was beside me.

'Are you okay? That's a pretty nasty smash.'

'Yes, I'm just a bit shaky, that's all. I'm on my way to pick up a friend from work.'

'You can come over to my house and ring from there'

I hesitated. As if he could read my mind he spoke.

'Come and meet my wife and the kids. We'll get you sorted.'

I breathed out. He didn't seem like a weirdo. We ran the gauntlet across traffic to his house. His wife offered me a cup of tea while his two children looked me up and down. I rang the RACV and the refuge where I worked. Another worker could pick me up.

'So what do you do?' I asked as I settled on the couch with my tea.

'I drive a bus for a Christian school.'

I sat up. 'I work for a Christian youth organisation,' I replied.

We laughed. We were both Christians. What were the chances of that? He told me it was a dangerous stretch of road with many accidents. He said God had put him in that place to help people like me in their moments of crisis.

Then the tow truck came and my lift. We said goodbye. I thanked him for his help. When I told my friend about him I couldn't remember his name. I could remember his address either, but I've never forgotten him. He was one of those angels sent to me.

An Inclusive Church
John Alexander Duthie

Since 2009 I've used a wheelchair for mobility purposes and experienced exclusion. It comes in the forms of steps instead of ramps, or the bathroom having insufficient space for my wheelchair and me. It also has occurred in churches, including a visit to watch a musical.

We arrived early to find a suitable location, and my three family members sat on the end of a row. It allowed me to sit next to them. A member of the church's 'welcome team' said hello to my family, then suggested another viewing location. They wanted me to move to a designated area reserved for people in wheelchairs. There were two problems 1) it was at the back of the church 2) only one member of my family could sit with me.

I thanked them for their suggestion and proceeded to sit in the original location, as our family wanted to sit together. Another member of the 'welcome team' approached me and told me that I couldn't sit at the end of the aisle. I was a fire hazard and would cause people to get burnt or die in a fire. After looking around and observing wide aisles, and families with prams that must also be OH&S hazards not being 'welcomed', I asked the person to go 'welcome' someone else. My family enjoyed the musical, and I wondered why the church treated people in wheelchairs so poorly. I also questioned why the regular worshippers in wheelchairs agreed to be herded into one area, and why they had to sit in the back of the church?

Another example of an exclusive church was a Christian men's conference called 'Man Up'. Upon arrival, I wasn't able to enter the building, as a door blocked the ramp, and they had to spend time looking for the key. At least they had a ramp, so that's nothing to complain about. During the morning tea break I asked to use the accessible toilet. I received confused looks on the faces of the regular church members.

I asked, 'Where can I go to the toilet?'

Their answer shocked me. 'We used to have a disabled toilet, but we needed more toilets for the women of the church'.

The lack of a suitable facility was a violation of the DDA (Disability Discrimination Act). A female church member ensured the women's toilets were clear, and I squeezed into a cubicle to urinate. So at a conference, which was held to help men 'Man Up', I was forced to use the women's toilets. I asked if the church had any members in wheelchairs and it wasn't a surprise the answer was 'no'. Given the exclusions, they may as well put up a sign that read, 'people in wheelchairs not welcome here'.

I spent over a year in rehabilitation following my accident, and would often eat lunch in a church cafe that was behind the hospital. Later, my daughter attended their youth group, followed by me attending worship and my son going to youth as well. The church people included PWD (people with disabilities) in the community of believers. I became involved in commencing a new branch of the church, and the minister decided to advertise the new location. He appeared in a video, letting us know the new address, and mentioned 'just come up the stairs'. Immediately, I was shocked that I would be excluded, as well as other people in wheelchairs and those that used other mobility devices. What made the situation worse is that the people affected were told via social media, instead of being contacted directly. I quickly shared my thoughts with other people in the church, and a few made comments such as, 'Stop complaining' or, 'It's only temporary'.

I wondered what the Bible said about disabilities. Unfortunately, Google sent me to a passage in Leviticus 21:17-23, which said:

'No man who has any defect may come near: no man who is blind or lame, disfigured or deformed; no man with a crippled foot or hand, or who is a hunchback or a dwarf, or who has any eye defect, or who has festering or running sores or damaged testicles. No descendant of Aaron the priest who has any defect is to come near to present the food offerings to the Lord. He has a defect; he must not come near to offer the food of his God.'

Can you imagine a church that placed an advertisement to fill a vacant position, which specially discounted people with

An Inclusive Church

disabilities? I doubt it would happen, and if it did, there would be a public outcry, which would make the church change its attitude. They might even be in breach of the DDA (Disability Discrimination Act).

I jumped to the New Testament and focused on Jesus. Given a few experiences in church and the passage in Leviticus, I wondered whether Jesus was inclusive. I read that Jesus spoke to women, children PWD. The religious authorities of his day kept their distance from these three groups. Jesus even healed a few PWD, and I found 41 verses that mentioned this.

'Great crowds came to him, bringing the lame, the blind, the crippled, the mute and many others, and laid them at his feet; and he healed them.' (Matthew 15:30)

'Yet the news about him spread all the more, so that crowds of people came to hear him and to be healed of their sicknesses.' (Luke 5:15)

'Aware of this, Jesus withdrew from that place. A large crowd followed him, and he healed all who were ill.' (Matthew 12:15)

'When Jesus landed and saw a large crowd, he had compassion on them and healed their sick.' (Matthew 14:14)

Back in the 1980s, the acronym WWJD ('What Would Jesus Do') was a famous catchphrase in churches. It seemed to me that Jesus was inclusive, and so should churches be. In my church, the response from the lead pastor was terrific, and he acknowledged the exclusion of people in wheelchairs. And he wants to make it easy for PWD to be involved in the life of the church. 18.5% of the population have a disability, but it seems that less than this percentage are involved in a church. If churches could be more inclusive for PWD, then possibly we could see more PWD during worship.

A Stranger Passing Through
Maria Rudolph

The Ghan made its way into Adelaide Railway Station. It had taken three glorious days filled with a lot of red soil up to the horizon, to get to South Australia's capital from humid Darwin. After six months of backpacking around Australia as a German backpacker, I had become a seasoned traveller. A new city and fresh adventures lay before me. It was too early in the morning for check-in at my hostel. Instead, I began walking around the streets to get a feel for this unknown place. A small sign pointing down Flinders Street caught my eye – 'German Club'. Filled with curiosity as to how such a thing existed 14,500 kilometres away from my home country, my steps led me down that street. I started noticing beautiful church buildings. Mostly, their doors were shut. But when I passed one with a wide open front portal, my feet took me up the stairs to have a peek inside. A handful of people went about decorating the front area. A smiling couple approached me and we started a friendly conversation. We bonded over laughs about their experience in an East German police station and my tales about Australian Outback roadhouses. They soon invited me to their house for dinner. Free food. That is music to the ears of a poor backpacker! Next thing, they also asked me to come along to Sunday worship at that church. I instantly agreed and then felt a bit bewildered – I had never been to a church service before. But after months of travelling around on my own, there had been stranger invitations than this one. It was worth finding out more.

When Sunday morning arrived, butterflies in my tummy accompanied the stroll back to the pretty church building. In anticipation, I slipped into one of the back pews and watched the service unfold. I was enthralled. It was unlike anything I had heard and seen before. There was beautiful music and singing and lots of words said back and forth between a pastor at the front and people looking back toward an altar set up with candles and shiny silverware, all to the backdrop of big stained glass windows. I thought of all the times I had visited church buildings. Never had I seen what happens in there in context.

Minutes later, the woman who had invited me there sat down next to me and helped guide me through the songs and responses. As my lips formed the words printed on a sheet in front of me and as my voice tried to join in the unfamiliar melodies, tears started running down my cheeks. They wouldn't stop. It was perplexing that there seemed to be too many emotions in me that I could not contain at that moment. Yet a strange peace filled me at the same time and it became obvious that these weren't sad tears. In fact, I didn't want the service to end. There came a realisation that I had found something profound, something I had not even realised I had been looking for. Or maybe it had found me. Some kind of unknown void inside of me had been filled to the brim. And more, I had to know more about what this was, a hunger to learn was awakened.

When the service finished and I found my way back into reality, the kind woman invited me across the road to a congregational luncheon. More free food. Definitely the way to a backpacker's heart! The church hall was filled with happy activity. Along with plates full of Aussie icons like sausage rolls, sandwiches, cold meats and salads, the people received me like the lost daughter! We laughed, shared stories, ate, drank and laughed some more. As I made my way back to my hostel later in the afternoon, a bag full of leftovers dangling on my arm, I was resolved to return to that place and find out more. The emotions and tears, the strange peace, the hospitality and unassuming kindness I had received, all these spun around my head for days afterwards.

This was the beginning of a journey that took me back to that church Sunday after Sunday. The friendly couple who first made contact with me when I was a stranger passing through became like family. They shared their time, their daily activities with me − for some weeks I even lived in their house. That meant more free food than any backpacker could ever dream of, but much more than that, their trust in me and the patience with which they started to explain God's Word in conversation blew me away time and again. They introduced me to a multitude of other Christians and integrated me in to their family life.

Some weeks later, it became clear to me that what I wanted more than anything was to be baptised and to commit to this new way of life properly. The friendly couple would become my much loved Godparents. My life was changed forever the moment I set foot in that church as a curious backpacker. A tremendous paradigm shift within me flipped life as I knew it upside down and turned it on its head.

On a chilly yet sunny autumn morning, my feet ascended the steps through the wide open front portal of the church building that now felt like home. The people who smilingly greeted me had become like family. I made my way up to the baptismal font during that Sunday service on which I officially became a part of God's family through baptism. Another time of worship packed with emotions. It was the most unexpected thing to happen to this young German backpacker. It marked the beginning of the biggest adventure there is – life as a child of God.

It took me some more years before I eventually made it inside the 'German Club', but some detours are worth taking. By the time I sat at one of its rustic tables and was served a hearty meal accompanied by cheery brass music, I was a theological student and permanent resident of Adelaide married to an Australian. Not a stranger passing through anymore.

The Unlikely Tractor Pull
Lisa Holbrook

I had been planning the way my job interview was going to go for the last week. In my head I was funny, charming and had all the answers (well, spiritually at least). Working in ministry had been my goal while I was in high school, and now, at nineteen years old, I'd seen enough of the world to know that this is what I wanted to do for the rest of my life.

I received a call offering me a job interview working in school ministry at a small school in the Adelaide Hills. It had already been a big morning; I had become lost several times on the windy roads but I still managed to find the school. I was far too early and I didn't want to sit in the staff carpark for that long. Instead, I decided to pull over to the side of the road for a quick prayer session before going in to interview for The Best Job in The World.

Clunk.

I tried going forward, going backwards, accelerating... nothing worked. I was just spinning my wheels. My car seemed stuck in some kind of hole. I rocked the car back and forth, switching from drive to neutral. It worked the times I'd been bogged in sand, but, today, it seemed to be making things worse. So much for my quiet time with God! Being an older car I'd had my fair share of problems and bingles. I'd be back into my sacred quiet time once I figured out what to do.

As I climbed out of the car the scent of eucalyptus trees was instantly soothing. It was a good thing, too. I needed to calm down. On close inspection I realised that my front left tyre was wedged in a ditch. It was more of a trench than a ditch, but one which was hidden by long grass either side. As was the case invariably throughout my college years, I didn't have enough phone credit to call the RAA for a tow.

There was only one thing for it. I'd have to leave my sunny, warm, prayer sanctuary, stuck-in-a-ditch car and head over to the farmhouse across the road.

As I stumbled across the road I started to regret my outfit. I was overdressed for 8.30am in my impossibly high boots which I loved (until I started wearing them). I didn't think I'd be walking down a gravel driveway. It was fairly short walk, and I pressed the doorbell, hoping someone would be home.

The lady who answered the door smiled and said hello. When I explained about my car, and my lack of phone credit, and the RAA, she just laughed.

'It'll take them hours to get out here. I know a guy up the road who can pull you out.' I meekly followed her to the car, and we zipped back up the hill to another house.

'Can you help pull this lass out of the ditch across from my place?'

'How'd that happen?'

Now was probably the right time to explain to her that I was applying for The World's Best Job, but instead I just mumbled something about checking a map. Soon we trailed a tractor back to my car, which unceremoniously towed my car out of the ditch. The guy drove off in his tractor, the lady drove her car back to her house and I sat in my car again, right on the shoulder. I drove until I could safely perform a U-turn and then drove back up the hill to the school.

After all the mucking around I was still seven minutes early. A quick prayer – a thank you – and inside I went for the interview for The Best Job in The World. During the interview I tried to share what I could bring: the youth vibe, great at craft, Bible college student. And the panel showed me what they could bring: great little school, nice staff, not very much money, but enough to cover petrol there and back. A school tour quickly showed me what I could be getting in to – or maybe, what God could be getting me into. Despite the tractor and the ditch this morning, I thought the school would be worth the commute a few days a week. The panel wrapped up the interview and I felt a sense of peace come over me. I didn't really want to leave.

As I shook hands with the school principal, I prayed a prayer I had never prayed before. *Lord, I want to work here. But, if I'm not the right person, I hope that you have someone awesome in mind.* I told the principal what happened with the tractor and the ditch, and he laughed, and gave me some pointers on taking a scenic route home.

Later that day I received the call. I was appointed. 'Are you sure?' I asked. 'Were there other applicants?'

'Yes, there were, but the panel wanted to employ you.'

I could barely believe it. How exciting, to be young and starting off in a role which had been my dream job. And how blessed to feel called to apply and then to be trusted enough in the position.

In my five years at The Best Job in The World, and in my ten in ministry to young people since, I found so often that God doesn't always call the equipped. He equips the called, and gives them the skills they need. Instead of being funny and charming, I'd said very little to the two complete strangers who helped pull my car out of a ditch. Instead of being the all-knowing spiritually mature person I hoped to be, it seemed the more I knew about God, the more I didn't understand.

I soon learned that I didn't have all the answers. Most of the time I didn't have any at all. Sometimes my job wasn't pulling anyone out of a ditch, I just had to sit there with them while God did his stuff. Sometimes it was bringing the fruit platter to the rescuers. And, sometimes, it was the unlikely and never-before-considered opportunity to allow myself to be rescued and wrapped up in love by the same people I'd been sent to minister to.

Story of My Life
Joyce Ling

It was a beautiful, sunny day. The trees were rustling slightly in the soft wind and the condominium was quiet and peaceful, perfect for a leisurely walk. My Mum was doing so, taking me and my sister, Dorcas, as well. I was about one or two years old, and Dorcas was two years older than me. There was a huge swimming pool surrounded by our condominium with three different levels of baby pools that had slides and stairs connecting them. We were strolling around, enjoying the gentle breeze and the scenic view, when my other sister, Grace, had problems doing her math homework and called from our house for Mum to help her. So Mum called me and Dorcas to go inside as well, but we stubbornly insisted on remaining outside. After much inefficacious persuading, Mum gave up trying to negotiate with us and instructed us to just stay around the first level and not to go near the pools. Then she went back to the house.

After helping Grace with her math, Mum went to clean up the house and wash the dishes. When doing so, she suddenly felt something bothering her in her heart. She felt like God was speaking to her, urging her to check on us. Feeling that something was wrong, Mum obeyed God's voice and rushed outside to see if we were alright.

Running outside, she paused. Her anxious eyes scanned her surroundings. There was no sign of me and my sister. Mum's heart throbbed painfully as she frantically called out our names in desperation. What could have happened to us? Were we in trouble? Did we need help? She simply couldn't imagine the possibilities of the situations we could be in. Then suddenly, she heard a little voice calling out. It was Dorcas' voice. It sounded like it came from the second level. Panic-stricken, Mum dashed to the slide that lead down to the pool on the second level. Her eyes focused on a terrifying scene.

Dorcas was standing on the edge of the pool, calling out with a calm voice. Mum's eyes darted in the direction she was looking, and they fell on a little figure floating face-down in the water. With a sharp gasp of horror, Mum realised that it was me in the pool! Even though the pool was very shallow, I couldn't stand up and balance myself because the nappy I was wearing prevented me from doing so and caused me to float horizontally with my face in the water. Dorcas was at the side, trying to call to me to get up and out of the water and not understanding why I didn't respond. Mum leaped down the stairs leading to the second level, not caring whether she would injure herself or break her legs skipping the steps of the stairs, and splashed into the shallow pool immediately. She lifted my motionless body from the water and quickly turned me over. My face was dark blue because I had not been able to breathe for the past few minutes. I was still not breathing and had no response when my Mum picked me up, so she quickly brought me and Dorcas back to the house.

Mum rushed me to the bathroom, turned on the taps, and faced the shower head towards me, showering me with hot water. Then she kept rubbing my body to warm me up, and patted my back vigorously to make me vomit out the water I had taken in. But I showed no sign of response. Mum pressed on, not giving up and worked hard to keep me alive, at the same time fervently praying to God for his healing hand to be upon me. Suddenly and finally, to her utter relief, I vomited out the water and burst out crying. Grateful and relieved, Mum hugged me close, thanking God for keeping me alive. A few more minutes in the pool and I'd have been gone.

This story has always amazed me, and whenever Mum tells it to me, I'm always astounded as to why and how God saved my life. I've always questioned why God would preserve my life, and therefore wondered what it is in my life that is so important. Is there something special in store for my future? In the end, I concluded that I believe God urged my Mum to go out there and save me for a special reason. I may not know what it is now, but I know that he has a purpose for my life. He kept me alive so that I can fulfil his will. Therefore, I am ready to use my life as a tribute to serve him, and share my miraculous testimony to glorify his name!

Confessions of a Realist

Emily Maurits

86 days, 10 operations and plenty of easily manageable prayers.

This is how long my teenage sister has been an inpatient at the Children's Hospital, Level 2: Neurology Ward.
The diagnosis? A slow-growing but large brain tumour.
The solution? Cut it out.
Simple.
Except nothing ever is. Hello, surgical complications.
Hello, Desperation.
Perhaps somewhere in this sprawling continent there lives an Exceptionally Insightful Individual who is able to look beneath my shaved scalp and swinging gypsy skirts and label me a 'realist'.
If there is, and if they did, they would be correct. Smack bang on the money. That is, if 'realist' means too afraid to pray big, impossible prayers. If 'realist' means too afraid to hope.
The problem is, I'm tired of being a 'realist' and sick of playing life safe. 89 days and 10 operations too tired. It's time to live up to my radical hairstyle… or maybe just my recently-tested faith.
I've never been a maths whizz, but the numbers are crunchable. If my sister is going to be healed before Christmas, I'm running out of time.

It's eleven days until the 25th, yet as a family we exchange gifts on Christmas Eve… so that only leaves ten days. The transition from institution to home is not an easy one, so she would need to be discharged at least two days before the 24th in order to settle in. This leeway would also give my parents and me time to construct some form of 'Christmas'.
My calculations clunk to a conclusion. The 22nd of December.
Eight days away.
I look down at the comatose body on the hospital bed, swathed in white blankets, held together by an invisible tincture of drugs, will

and Spirit, and a much more visible array of drooping tubes and blinking monitors.

How long does a miracle take? Is eight days enough? The 'realist' in me thinks not. I open my mouth anyway.

Please Lord.

It hurts to pray. Hurts like it does when you throw a comment into a conversation and have no clue whether you'll be met with agreement or confused silence. Hurts like it does when you offer companionship but wonder if you'll find yourself alone after the party.

Bring her home on the 22nd of December.

I ache with the sheer impossibility of the words. Now I've spit them into being, what will I do if the morning of the 23rd dawns and my sister's bedroom remains empty?

This is not the prayer of a realist. What would the Exceptionally Insightful Individual say if they saw me now?

99 days, 11 operations and one impossible prayer.

I wake on the 22nd to the sound of a million coins falling onto pavement. A glance out the window shows the rain is accompanied by wind strong enough to throw the branches of our huge white gumtree into disarray.

In a film this would be a carefully placed premonition, complete with threatening piano notes. Real life is rarely so obliging, but I still feel giddy. My body shakes with that peculiar type of trembling ecstasy which follows an all-nighter and a bad knock-knock joke. Yet it's not a punchline I'm waiting for. It's a lifeline.

As I pull on my blue-and-white skirt and smooth down an already smooth waistband, a little-used voice whispers that perhaps today will be The Day. Perhaps God will give me my miracle.

Don't be ridiculous, a far more well-oiled voice replies. God doesn't work that way. Not for you, not today. You're wasting your time, your energy, your hope.

Can hope be wasted? Is it a single use item like a sticky band-aid or a disposable face-mask? Or is it something multi-purpose, like washable bandages and air-purifiers? Better yet, is there a hope which comes with a life-time guarantee? If so, I'll get six, thanks. I'll even sign up to the 'we promise no spam' promotional email!

I walk downstairs.

'What did they say?'

Mum presses the 'end-call' button and rests the phone in her lap. These past 99 days have given our landline a workout. No longer is it the final frontier: 'Beware. Out there be marketers!' Instead if you asked, it could babble about tearful ten pm calls and sober six am consents for surgery. It would probably complain over the endless monotony of conversations beginning, 'How are you?' and concluding with litanic variations of, 'We love you.'

'She had raisin toast for breakfast and woke early when the nurse –'

'Good,' I derail Mum's response and set about changing direction. 'Did they say whether she can come home today?'

It's not the question of a realist.

Mum frowns. 'Home? Of course not. Perhaps by Christmas Eve, but even then…'

My prayer had been a secret. Realists do not have the liberty of molding hope into sentences.

Outside in the storm the gumtree screams with primal fury. Inside near the phone my faith stutters through silent syllables.

What are you doing, God? I thought – I hoped –

It's okay. The realist in me re-asserts herself. Your faith doesn't require miracles. God still cares. Not everyone gets a showy display of heavenly love.

The words may be reasonable, but they bring no comfort.

99 days, 11 operations and one far too impossible prayer.

The nurse looks from my sister to me and flicks her short blonde hair behind an ear. 'Once the Endocrine team signs off, are you happy to take her home this afternoon?'

Happy. Am I *happy?*

Oh Lord. The nurse's casual question reverberates against the walls in my soul and they begin to crumple. In fear I try to hold them upright. I am a realist. I have to be certain.

'Are you sure?'

The nurse nods. 'We'll call to check on you and she'll have to have follow up appointments with the various teams within two to six weeks of discharge…' She continues through prescriptions and descriptions and medical-predictions, and we've heard it all before… or at least I hope we have, because neither of us are listening.

I let the walls dissolve to dust. My sister's eyes shine.

99 days, eleven operations and one answered prayer.

It's the 22nd of December and my sister is coming home.

Three years, seven months and one miracle.

Perhaps somewhere in this sprawling continent there lives an Exceptionally Insightful Individual who is able to look beneath my shoulder length curls and professional black slacks and label me a 'realist'.

If there is, and if they did, they'd be right. Smack bang on the money. That is, if 'realist' means no longer afraid to pray impossible prayers. If 'realist' means one who has witnessed a miracle and lives to tell the tale.

Three years, seven months and one miracle.

That's how long it's been since my sister came home from the Children's Hospital, Level 2: Neurology Ward, healed of a brain tumour.

Hello, unexplainable cure.

Hello, Hope.

One Blue Arrow at a Time

Naomi Currie

'Wait a sec,' I puff. 'Give me a mo to catch my breath.' I sit down gingerly on a convenient boulder and pull out my water-bottle. My sister and father nod without comment. It's the umpteenth time I've requested a breather.

'It's a hot day,' I say. Again my family nod. It is mid-April in the Flinders Ranges. The calendar might claim it is mid-autumn, but this year it is simply the continuation of a long, hot, summer and widespread drought. My shirt is soaking wet with sweat where the straps of my backpack sit and my lips taste of salt. We have left most of the trees, and all of the shade, down in the valley. The trees up here are simply a smattering of leaves glued onto dry sticks, providing a little dappled shade and no respite from the sun's glare, interspersed with shaggy shrubs that are covered with malicious hidden thorns.

There is an arrow stencilled in blue paint on my boulder. I follow the direction of the pointer, with my eyes, across and up the rocks to a second blue arrow. There will be hundreds of the blue arrows and reflectors. Together they mark out a trail that will lead us all the way to the top of St Mary's Peak (*Ngarri Mudlanha*), the highest point in the Ikara-Flinders Ranges National Park, and about 1,168 metres above sea level.

At some points the trail is a flat, clearly defined path signposted every two hundred metres; at others, it is more of a scramble up a landscape where the vegetation has been ripped out randomly to expose piles of weathered rock.

'How far up do you reckon we are?' my sister asks.

I squint at the heat-haze and wispy cloud to find the top of the ridge. 'Maybe halfway up? But I read that you have to go up and over this ridge, then across a saddle between two ridges and up the other one. You can't see the peak from here.'

'Oh. That's encouraging.'

'Well, there's the next blue arrow over there.' We start climbing again, using hands and feet to pull ourselves up the steep bits.

Some minutes later we see movement ahead of us. 'There's someone coming down,' I hiss over my shoulder. 'Keep left.' It's an idiotic instruction; the trail is only one-person in width. We stop and move to the side so the stranger can pass.

He's wearing all the proper hiking gear; the khaki-green floppy hat with fly-veil; the sand-coloured cargo pants, with zips to turn them into shorts; and the long-sleeved shirt that shouts '50+ UV protection' and 'ultra-breathable' fabric. He has the lightweight backpack with inbuilt water-cooler and sipping tube, the sturdy hiking boots and a spiked hiking pole. He looks like he has just stepped out of an outdoor adventure store catalogue.

I am suddenly conscious I am wearing an ordinary, short-sleeved top, a $10 floppy hat and sport-shoes designed for a netball court. I'm carrying several water-bottles, but they're emblazoned with sponsor's logos and were free handouts from some business promotion.

'G'day. Thanks.' He pauses for a moment. 'Good luck!' Is he just being nice, or implying that we need it?

'Is the view worth it?' My dad asks. Goodness, do we really want to hear the answer?

'Oh, I didn't get all the way to the top. Would have, of course, but I rolled my ankle. Thought it best to head back and leave the full climb for another day.'

My dad responds politely and my sister sympathetically. After a brief conversation, the man continues down the trail and we are climbing again. In silence.

If somebody with all the right gear and probably lots of experience only made it part-way… what hope do we have? Maybe we shouldn't have been so eager. Maybe we should have waited until another time, perhaps coming back when we have done other things first. When we have more experience. When we have all the right-looking equipment.

My backpack feels heavy and my mind keeps repeating dully, 'Foothold to the left, handhold to the right, he didn't make it, so why should we? Foothold to the left…'

Suddenly my dad starts laughing. 'You know who that man's like? Remember Pilgrim's Progress?'

Vaguely. Some old book about a man called Christian going on a journey. A very long metaphor or allegory or something.

'Well,' Dad continues, 'I'm calling that man we met Mr Discouragement.'

'Huh?'

'Oh, it's all in the story. Anyway, the point was that Christian met all these people at different times who tried to stop him continuing the journey. Like that man we met. That man might not have meant to be discouraging, but he certainly was!'

'That's right!' My sister chimes in. 'And Christian had to ignore them and keep going! Well that's what we're going to do too!' She strikes a pose, fist thumps the air and almost falls off a rock she is balancing on.

'If you break your leg, we certainly won't make it to the peak!' But I begin to laugh too. My backpack feels suddenly lighter and my legs have more energy. We *are* going to make it top of the mountain, I know we will.

An hour later, that confidence is shaken. We're lost. Rather thoroughly. Oh, we know we are partway up a mountain, but wherever did the trail go?

Not that long ago, we were following a dirt track running parallel to the ridge top, a brief hiatus between climbing segments. Somehow, we must have deviated onto a goat track, something that started out looking like a true pathway, but ended irrevocably in a wall of thorns. We tried to cast out a little; suddenly there were dry dirt tracks running everywhere. Yet all of them ended abruptly in rocks or vegetation, certainly not a trail.

I reach into my backpack and pull out my map. 'The problem with this map is that I don't know where we are on it.'

'Isn't that obvious?' My sister asks sarcastically.

'Oh! Well, yes.' The map is the one provided by the visitor information centre at Wilpena Pound. It has no topography marked on it, just a dashed line wriggling through a flat blob of green. 'I can tell you where we're not,' I say, perking up a little, pointing to the carpark where we started the trail.

'Thanks. Oh,' she says excitedly, 'I've got a maps app on my phone. Let's try that!'

We peer at her phone screen. A little red marker appears. 'That's us! Zoom in!' It takes time for the marker to reposition itself. We wait and wait, but nothing changes. There is simply a little red marker against a green background. The trail is not marked. Topographical features are not marked. She tries a different app, but it tells her there are no pre-downloaded maps of the area. So that is that.

No point staying where we are. 'Do you want to try going up or down?' Dad asks. If we go down, surely we will intersect the trail somewhere as it runs along the side of the ridge. If we go up... firstly, it looks very steep, secondly, we could miss the trail by hundreds of metres, depending on where the track actually crosses the ridge.

Yet I hate the idea of going downwards. To have to admit that trying to find our own way up will not work and that we need to go back down, to where we last saw the path. I struggle against the logical solution, then capitulate. 'Okay, let's go down.'

Within half-an-hour we are back on the trail. 'It's quite embarrassing, really,' my sister says, as we walk fast along the flat – and well defined – section of track. 'We safely navigated all the blue arrows, those bits where you could very easily get lost. And then stray off this!'

'Maybe we got too cocky and stopped paying attention.'

'Not doing that again!'

We don't. For the next couple of hours we follow the blue arrows all the way to the top of the mountain. And, yes, the view and the satisfaction of accomplishment were worth it.

* * *

It is eighteen months later. I am still following the blue arrows. Sometimes I can see a line of them ahead; other times I must climb in faith, precisely in the direction of the one pointer I can see. Sometimes I stray and must stop and find the way again.

One Blue Arrow at a Time

I don't know precisely which of the rocks I see scattered around me I must climb. I can't pinpoint my location on a map. But I know that the blue arrows are there, painted in my life by the hand of God. And they will lead me all the way to the top of the mountain.

The Circle of Love
Liisa Grace-Baun

In December 1964 I was born to an alcoholic in the town of Imatra, Finland.

She gave birth to another daughter a few years before me who was taken by my biological grandmother in the hope of a better life. However when I was born my grandmother said 'I will not take in another, you will have to find somewhere else for her'.

My biological mother was a qualified nurse and a nearby nursing home offered her residence there with me on the condition that she work there. She did this for seven months before suddenly disappearing, leaving me behind with a note in my cot saying that she wasn't able to live like this anymore. Rumour was that she had gone back on the ships, trading as a prostitute.

A neighbouring family cared for me until I was nine months old. They had agreed to take me in until my mother was found however after two months they were unable to keep me any longer. Social Services intervened and approached a family with six children who lived on a farm with the request to care for me.

Laila asked her youngest son how he felt about having a little sister and with no objection from him I was taken to that family the following day. Laila grew to love me as her own and the six children all embraced me as their new little sister.

Laila's husband struggled to operate his own business and eventually went bankrupt. Soon after this, Laila saw an advertisement in the local paper for migration to Australia, promoting employment opportunities. She proceeded to put in an application and the family was approved to migrate to Adelaide, Australia.

The excitement from the family couldn't be contained and each family member began selling or giving away most of their belongings in preparation to move to the other side of the world. The time came to apply for passports and Laila was told that she was unable to apply for my passport as I was not legally her child.

The Circle of Love

She began the search for my biological mother who I had not seen since the day she abandoned me four years earlier.

My biological mother was located in a town called Hamina, where she was now married with a one-year-old son. When approached with the request to allow Laila and her husband to legally adopt me, she denied it and instead took me back.

On the day I was collected, Laila was distraught and went to a neighbour's house as she couldn't bear to say goodbye. I didn't understanding what was happening. My biological mother and her husband were strangers to me and I longed for Laila, for the family that I was truly part of. Laila had given me a doll which my biological mother took from me and gave to my one-year-old brother. Day after day I was beaten with a crown of thorns that hung on the wall and then put outside in the snow naked. Her husband would have his way with me. I became paralysed in fear.

After several months, a neighbour reported to the police that I was being left outside naked in the freezing cold. Soon after that I was taken away from them and placed into an orphanage in Hamina. I recall the cook having a warmth to her which reminded me of Laila, however the older boys that resided there took pleasure in tormenting me physically and sexually. Night after night, I would fold my hands in prayer as Laila had taught me to do, and I sobbed to be with Laila whom I was missing immensely.

Meanwhile, Laila and the family had migrated to Australia. After several months Laila received news from her sister that I had been placed in an orphanage. She immediately wrote a letter to Social Services in Finland, pleading to adopt me. Court proceedings went ahead and after twelve months, at the age of five, Laila and her husband became my legal parents.

The Australian government paid for my airfare and I still remember being on the big aeroplane travelling far away from what I knew as home.

Upon arrival at Adelaide Airport, my beautiful mother Laila and the rest of the family greeted me, as well as television crews to report it.

Years later Laila told me how her heart ached as I was no longer speaking when I arrived here, yet I had been speaking fluently when I lived with them in Finland. I recall being completely withdrawn. I was not able to articulate the trauma I had endured as a child, but which I was healed from in my adult years, by God's healing grace.

Life in Australia was unstable. My adoptive father was a violent alcoholic. My mother and I often had to flee in the night and run to my sister's house for refuge.

Laila was not an affectionate woman nor was she expressive with her emotions, but deep inside I knew she loved me. I recently came across an article that she had written to a magazine in Finland soon after the victory of adopting me, in which she expressed that she loved me more than her biological children.

When I had children of my own, they became exceptionally close to Laila. She was their 'Mummi' which means 'grandma' in Finnish. She loved my children dearly and they taught her to be affectionate and expressive with their love. I nurtured them from birth so they were naturally affectionate and loving with their Mummi.

The past few years I cared for my precious mother daily. I took her to appointments, cleaned and cooked for her and helped in whichever way she needed. She often asked me why I was the only one who would do this, and I'd tell her each time that it was because I will never forget that she did it for me when I came into this world.

Last year I faced the difficulty of placing her into a nursing home as she refused to come and live with my husband and me. I saw her every day and I grieved with her for the independence she was losing.

Earlier this year she was admitted to hospital and on day three a code blue was called. I was convinced we were losing her. On one of my visits she said 'please Liisa, go home and look after your family, if it's my time to go there is nothing you can do, just let me go'. I refused to hear that and instead reminded her of the tickets we had for a cruise on the lake as well as tickets to go and see the

The Circle of Love

Ten Tenors in May. I told her that I would not let her go yet. She smiled a weary smile and softly said 'ok'. I told my mum that I love her, and for the first time in my life I heard her say those words back. Every day since then we would say to each other 'I love you'.

At the end of April her specialist told me that she was at the end of her life and that we didn't have long with her due to heart and kidney failure. From that day onwards I would stay at the nursing home with her most nights. My husband, children, grandchildren and I showered her with love daily. I reminded her continually that I would be with her to the very end just as she was with me from the very beginning.

Daily her condition worsened and on the last day of May I felt compelled to let her know that she could go now. I buried my head in her hair as I cried and told her how much I love her while also telling her the things I thanked her for. We had been on the cruise and seen The Ten Tenors. As my cheek pressed against hers I felt my tears on her face, and with much anguish and sorrow I said 'Mum you can go now, Jesus is waiting for you. Just take his hand and your mum's hand, they are both waiting for you now'. She hadn't been responsive for several days but the most amazing thing happened. She replied with 'ahuh' so I knew that she had understood me.

Later that night as we huddled around her singing Amazing Grace and playing her favourite songs, her breathing became shallow. We listened to the song 'You Raise Me Up' and at the end of the song she gently took her last breath. I cried for my mum in Finnish 'Aiti, Aiti, Aiti'. Panic came over me when I realised there would be no more card games, no more cooking days, no more singing, no more stories or laughter, and no more 'I love you's, but she will live in my heart forever.

Vessel
Rebecca Abdel-Nour

I rise when the first smudges of light colour the eastern horizon. The household is still. I wrap my robe tightly around myself and silently cross the passageway to the bathroom with the slow, heavy movements of one still detaching from the heavy embrace of sleep. The alternative universe of dreaming isn't easily left behind.

The chipped, worn, tiles that have been here since the seventies are cold beneath my feet. I quake, but the coldness seems to originate from within. I stare down at my toes for some moments, mustering the courage to take the next step. In the end, it is the cold that drives me forward and I step onto the bathroom scales with my eyes closed. The feeling is hard to describe. There is some solace in not knowing, in being, for a few moments at least, unquantifiable. Suspended in uncertainty. But ultimately there is much more comfort in knowing. Seizing. Controlling. Being the master of my own temple.

My eyes open. A two hundred gram surplus. I let out a shaky breath. *That stupid apple.* I'd feared this would be the case. Worse than the weight gain was the lapse in willpower that led to it. No fruit today then.

The living area with the tiny offset kitchen is quiet. I prefer rising to eat alone. I can count the number of times I chew (thirteen) before swallowing without distraction. I can savour the taste, the touch, the texture. It is a hedonistic routine. A ritual. A rite.

I carefully weigh my cereal and measure the skim milk. In a few gulps I consume a tall glass of water before starting to eat. The water is useful in taking the edge off my hunger. As I chew, a sense of unease sweeps in like a draught. Snatches of conversation from yesterday's appointment resurface unbidden. In my mind's eye I see him leaning forward towards me, pushing up his glasses with his index finger and fixing me with a sombre stare. *Emaciation... Lowered body mass index... compromised cardiac function.* The awareness that something is wrong had been hovering for some time. It had been like a distant light on the far side of my consciousness. Tilting and floating like a sun-bleached buoy on the edge of the horizon, indistinct. Indistinct, that is, until yesterday. Now the issue is glaringly in focus. I see it but no way out if it.

I pull on my track pants and sneakers and write a short note to my roommate, letting her know I have gone for a run. I push my earbuds in and try to rouse myself into action with a favoured playlist. The July morning is relentlessly cold. The sky is white-grey and inviolable. It is Sunday morning and the shops are still closed, but as I jog past them, every glass storefront becomes an unwelcome mirror. Tarnished gold leaves crunch underfoot. My breath is vapour, released into the frigid world in iambs.

At the stoplights I run on the spot, frustrated by the delay. I watch as the road gradually becomes reinhabited. Couples step out of cars and stride through doorways into the cafes of King William Road. The first wave. Early birds. They lounge in bistro seating receiving steaming plates and cups, some hold hands across the table. The contrast to my own Sunday routine is glaring. Despite the exertion and the physical kilometres covered, I still can't shake the sense that I am standing still, or worse yet, slowly sinking.

I finish my run and shower hastily, looking at my body as little as possible, wincing at the softness of my thighs, my stomach. I let the steam envelop me until I am disembodied, beyond the world of matter.

Wrapped in a thick towel I emerge from the bathroom. My roommate appears in the doorway of her bedroom. Her bed-hair gives her the profile of a crested cockatoo. She peers at me, still in my towel and raises her eyebrows, disapproval and concern angling for domination.

'Morning.'

I return the greeting and shuffle away from under her scrutiny, emerging minutes later from my bedroom in an oversized jumper and loose track-pants. By now she is buttering hot toast. She sits in the old armchair where the morning sunlight enters the room most stridently, an anthology of some kind spread over her knee, reading as she eats.

'Let's go to the evening service,' she suggests, eyes still glued to the page before her. 'I'm too swamped to go out this morning.'

'Sure. Works for me.'

She looks up momentarily from her book, 'I'm still working on that Dransfield paper. There are a few paragraphs to go.' She takes a bite of toast. 'His best stuff is about addiction. Listen to this,' she wipes her mouth briefly before reading aloud, 'Once you have become a drug addict/ you will never want to be anything else…' Isn't that poignant?'

The poetry takes a few moments to sift and settle, as poetry does.

I slowly nod. 'What do you think it means?'

'Well,' she takes another bite of toast and washes it down with iced coffee before responding. 'I guess it means that addiction can narrow your perspective and make your world become small.'

I spend the afternoon baking banana bread. I cook often. It is a way of enjoying food vicariously through the sight, the smell and the enjoyment of others. My roommate eats enthusiastically but I don't eat at all. I know now this isn't *normal*, it isn't healthy, but I have no idea how to begin to change. The thought of altering my ways, breaking my rules or changing my habits makes me break out in an instant sweat. I drop off the left-overs to a friend who lives down the road. I won't feel a sense of ease now until they are out of the house.

When I return home I am listless. Again, memories of yesterday's conversation return to me. The wrinkle in his brow as he spoke with earnestness. Snatches of the conversation echo in my mind. *Needs to be a turning point…a number of treatment options available…*

I am restless. Uneasy. The room seems to shrink.

'I am going for a walk,' I call to my roommate.

There is a pause. 'Okay.'

As the sun sets I ready myself for the evening service. *How long will the service run for? What will I eat afterwards? Soup and salad with perhaps some fish?* If I can consume this and nothing else for the rest of the day I'll be safe. I wonder what percentage of my thoughts revolve around food. I wonder what percentage don't.

I feel the cold more these days. It is difficult to leave the house now, when the sun withdraws and the cold radiates off the city surfaces like light, but I feel drawn to the church service today. I step out into the cold.

We enter the church and choose seats close to the back. The sound of conversation and laughter fills the room. The music soon begins and the lights fade. The melodies are soft tonight; the lyrics are like breathed prayers. I feel some of my tension slowly begin to dissipate.

Soon the singing comes to a close and an unfamiliar speaker introduces himself and begins to read from a passage of the Bible that I haven't heard since Sunday School. Intrigued, I listen as he recounts the story of Noah. It is a familiar narrative, and to begin with, the preacher's discourse is exactly as I would expect; he paints a picture of the violence of the inhabitants of the earth, explaining the need for renewal through the great flood. He tells of Noah's unique mission in constructing the ark to preserve his family, the courage he demonstrated in accepting the instructions of God, the contempt he faced from his peers. The story is stirring, soothing, familiar. I am surprised by the preacher's next words.

'Noah could not build the vessel however he wanted. God gave Noah guidance about *how* to build, in fact, he gave Noah the *exact dimensions* he needed to follow to ensure the vessel would last and do all it was designed to. Noah just had to believe God and respond in faith.'

The preacher's words are charged with purpose and they sink into me like rain. I lean back in my seat, remembering, once more, the conversation with my doctor the day before. He too had talked about building to last, about dimensions, sustenance and longevity. I am on the edge of my seat as the preacher closes his sermon with one last assertion: 'The vessel belonged to God and God knew how best to build to achieve his purpose.'

Good Out of the Bad

Leanne Chong

2018 ended really rough for me. I was hoping 2019 was going to be a better year. I was stressed, and my walk with God was really going nowhere. God didn't feel real to me at all.

However, God made something happen that restored my faith and trust in him.

Only two days after the new year, I had just come back from class. My mother walked into my room and told me something I thought would never happen. My cousin Natasha, who lives in another country, had been swimming in a pool. She was trying to see how many laps she could swim without coming up to take a breath. She successfully did a few laps. She was doing fine. Then she stopped swimming and sank to the bottom of the pool.

After a while, someone noticed her, pulled her out, and a swim coach at the pool administered CPR and was able to resuscitate her. But she was having seizures and grunting and was not really responding to anything. It was later discovered that she had been in the pool for six minutes and her lungs had filled with water. She was rushed to the hospital, put on a ventilator and also placed into an induced coma so her body could rest and heal.

At that time, when I heard the news, I didn't really know how bad it actually was and I didn't think about her much. I wish I cared more about her then. I was her cousin and her own cousin wasn't even thinking about her when she had nearly drowned.

When my family and I started to pray for her the next day, I cried. It was then that I realised how serious this was. One after another, the bad news kept coming. We were told she might have brain damage because her brain was deprived of oxygen for a long time, or that she may never recover.

I felt scared. I kept asking God why he would let something like that happen to her. Why he couldn't just instantly heal her. Jesus healed people on the spot in the Bible, why couldn't the same thing happen to Natasha? I felt that it was so unfair that God would let something like that happen to our family. I had so many questions that I wanted the answers to. God seemed so silent at that moment. I didn't understand.

Natasha and I used to talk about our interests, our struggles, our hopes and dreams, and what we wanted to become when we grow up. Now she might not be able to achieve her dreams just because of one small mistake. I was so angry at God. I was really angry.

I could focus only on her for days. Everything else did not matter to me. I felt guilty for not being there for her. I tried my best to keep praying for her without getting frustrated at God.

A few day later, she started regaining strength little by little, and she woke up a few times. When she was cleared of brain damage, I was still worried about her lungs. What if her lungs weren't strong enough? However, when doctors told us that her lungs were slowly healing and she would be fine, I was overjoyed.

I would get to see her again. We would get to talk and laugh together again. The relief I had was the best feeling ever. I felt joy slowly coming back into my life and God was so real to me at that point of time. I realised that sometimes we worry too much and forget that God has everything in his hands.

I also learned that sometimes God uses bad situations to bring out good things. Like in John 9, where Jesus healed a blind man, and his disciples asked him who sinned: him or his parents? And Jesus answered, 'Neither this man nor his parents sinned, but that the works of God should be revealed in him.' I know that God let this happen to Natasha because he wanted to let his works be shown in her.

It has been about six months since her incident. I've seen her only once but she is completely healthy and I am so thankful that she is okay. I know that God is protecting her. I'm actually very glad that God has taught me to trust in him because it made me continue growing again. This is the greatest miracle I have ever seen in my life.

Rebirth
Kylie Gardiner

Is this what it's like to lose your mind? I felt out of myself. Weird. Like an observer of my own life. I could walk down the street and see other people sitting outside cafés, laughing, sipping coffee and talking with friends, but it was like they were in a bubble and I was outside of it. I couldn't explain the feeling.

I sat in the doctor's waiting room, staring straight ahead, my husband next to me, our newborn in the baby carrier. An overwhelming sense of dread weighed on my whole body. Something was squeezing my insides. I kept telling myself things would get better once I got some sleep. I tried to hang on to positive thoughts. I could do this, I thought. I've just got to hang in there. But still I couldn't control the feelings.

As I sat there in the waiting room I feared I would be locked away. Do they still do that? I'm going to be locked away and I'll lose my baby. I'm so scared. I just want to hold her and feel normal again. I saw another woman with a pregnant belly across from me. I wanted to scream at her. Do you know what you're doing? Do you know what it will do to your mind?

Disconnected, I sat there. Crazy thoughts. My mind played over scenes from childhood, wondering if the seeds of my depression lay there. Was I the victim of some sort of abuse that I couldn't remember? Was I re-experiencing grief over the death of my Mum now that I had become a mum myself? Was I stuck in my grief from a previous premature stillbirth? I felt welded to the past. All my memories were dark. Please Lord, don't let my life end like this.

I looked down at my beautiful baby girl. I picked her up and held her. My love for her had not altered. I was thankful for that.

'You're a nervous first mum,' the doctor said. 'All new mothers feel like this but they just don't tell anyone. Mothers are the worst at lying about how they really feel.'

He gave me some sleeping pills. Told me to go back on the pill as this would level out the hormones. He echoed my obstetrician's advice that if you think you're going crazy then that's a good indication that you're not. This gave a moment's relief.

I had shocking insomnia. For me the day never ended. The only sleep I had was an hour or two from a sleeping tablet and I didn't want to get addicted to them. The more you took, the less you slept. How cruel was that. Other mums would relay stories of only getting five hours of sleep. Five hours! I was ravenous for that.

Ordinary moments of pleasure were taken away from me. To feel better I went for a massage but, even though I could feel the masseuse's hands on my skin, I could feel no pleasure from it. The memory of how it used to feel made me acutely aware of the losses in my life and that seemed to make it worse.

Our daughter was the most unsettled baby. The maternal and child health nurse said we'd been given the double whammy – reflux and colic. We were booked into a day clinic for unsettled babies. Kirrally would only sleep for twenty minute periods, even through the night. We were taught how to wrap our babies to help settle them. Kirrally did not settle. All day she was awake. The mothercraft nurse laughed and said she was officially the worst baby they'd ever had! She told me she would probably settle down in about three to four months. That was eternity to me.

I finally confessed to my maternal and child health nurse that I wasn't coping. She said to ring the mother/baby unit at the hospital. I could do a five day program there. Get some sleep and some time out for me. The nurse returned my call but said there was a three week waiting list. I broke down on the phone. I had this hope that I would be able to get in straight away and finally get some sleep. I didn't know if I'd be alive in three weeks. She asked me if I had any thoughts of harming myself or my baby. I said no. It freaked me out that someone could be asking that. It was not that I wanted to die so much as it was agony to live. I just wanted to be with Jesus. I was terrified that I would have my baby taken off me if they knew how awful I felt. A few days later the phone rang. They'd unexpectedly found me a spot. Thankyou, Lord.

But still I couldn't sleep. As a condition of my stay I had to see a psychiatrist. I was open to medication as a last resort so I started taking an anti-depressant but it gave me awful heart palpitations. I stopped taking it a day later as I couldn't bear the side effects. The one positive from the mother/baby unit was that Kirrally was examined by a paediatrician. He said she wasn't sleeping because her oesophagus was extremely inflamed. Her stomach muscle wasn't developed enough to stop the acid coming up and it was burning her throat. It was such a relief to find out what was wrong and that it wasn't my fault that she was so unsettled. She went on medication and was a completely different baby. Another answer to prayer.

I was still stuck on this question of why post-natal depression had happened to me. I'd wrangled teenagers in lunchtime programs. I'd dealt with difficult students as a teacher. I'd been on suicide watch with young people in the accommodation service where I'd lived as a youth worker. If I could handle those things, why couldn't I cope with being a mum? I would fixate on the question of why this had happened to me. I would journal any spare minute I had and constantly ruminate on it. Why had God allowed me to experience such lows? He taught me I had to surrender the need to understand.

I only told a few close friends how I was feeling as I was scared of being judged or told I lacked faith. Sometime later a doctor friend from church told me it was no reflection on my character if I had to go on medication. He had noticed me not eating when we were at their place for a meal. I'd lost a lot of weight and had no appetite. It gave me the permission I needed. After a visit to my GP I agreed to try another anti-depressant. This time the heaviness began to lift. I started to get more sleep. Three hours, then five and finally eight hours. I still felt wobbly. So we upped the medication. I hated being dependent on medication but God chose to use medication as part of my healing. As someone said to me, 'even Moses took his tablets!'

The U2 song 'Stuck in a Moment' had a special resonance for me too as I felt I was in that place but that this time would pass. It gave me much needed hope.

Fifteen years later the black dog will still nip at my heels but I try to look after myself and have some creative outlet. I've had to learn that God is with me in my situation. God has also given me rich relationships with others who have also suffered and allowed me to experience the deep sense of connection that comes with sharing your difficulties. I could feel unproductive with depression but it's then that I remind myself that God is more concerned with my character than my achievements.

After three years, when I was well again (but not the same), we finally felt ready to try for a brother or sister for Kirrally. Unfortunately I miscarried a baby boy at fourteen weeks who had many foetal abnormalities like our first child. After much prayer we decided that our family was complete. We chose to see our daughter as the miracle. We had two babies with many things wrong with them and they had gone to be with Jesus. Kirrally was perfectly formed in every way. Our special blessing from God.

I wanted to conquer depression. I wanted to be victorious. I wanted to come out of it praising God for a miraculous overnight healing and have an amazing testimony. I discovered it didn't quite work like that for me. But I have learned a deeper trust, and that, despite how I might feel, God is with me in my struggles. I learned there are times to hold on and times to let go. I cling to the promise that with God, no experience is ever wasted. There is always the hope of rebirth.

The Dress

Jane Owers

You can tell a lot about a persons by their shoes. Looking at me when I was 24 it was easy to see I was a struggling single mum who hated being cold. The only new clothes I bought were Kmart shoes and underwear. I was an avid op shopper with a good collection of jumpers and even a ski outfit for my daughter.

From the outside, the house I lived in with my daughter looked magnificent. It was two and a half stories high made with sandstone blocks some half a metre wide and windows two metres tall. Yet, inside, it was an empty building site with cement floors and no kitchen, freezing in winter. Basically it reflected me, trying to look presentable on the outside, hollow on the inside, craving warmth.

When I got tired of sleeping on a mattress that was home to a family of mice and needed a towel to cover the springs digging into me, I went back to work and then moved into a unit close to town. Going back to work got me a mattress but did not stop the daily struggle as I could only work part time. As a result, I still bought most of my clothes at op shops.

So when a good friend at work invited me to her wedding I had a problem. I already felt shame because when showing photos of my daughter and myself at work, colleagues pointed out that I was wearing my work shoes in the photo. At the time they were my only shoes and I was mortified. I now wanted to show everyone I could look good.

With a few months till the wedding I bought an embroidery kit for only $20 that I knew my friend would love and then spent hours embroidering the picture. With each stitch of tapestry I sewed for my friend I dreamed of my ideal dress that would make me look special. My dream dress was midnight blue, long sleeves to keep my arms warm and velvet because I love texture. I looked all over town for a dress close to my dream but found nothing. When I picked up the tapestry from the framer and only two weeks till the wedding I found out it had cost another $50. That blew my budget and any chance of fulfilling my dream.

The Dress

It was time to talk to my father in heaven who had promised me good things. I explained all my feelings, my shame for how I had let him down and how I really did not think I could get to be a better person but how I really needed him and his help to stop my embarrassment with my work colleagues.

The next day I went op shopping and there was my dream dress. Midnight blue, long sleeved velvet dress my size and hand made. It was only God who knew of my dream and only God who could provide that dress. Even though he knew all my thoughts and faults God still loved me enough to fulfil my dreams.

Isn't it time you told YOUR story?

This year, nine writers have shared in $3,000 in prize money and exposure for their stories.

In 2020, will you have YOUR story ready?

There are three categories for your Story of Life.

Tabor Stories of Life (1000 to 1500 words)

Eternity Matters Short Stories of Life (up to 500 words)

Lutheran Education Young Stories of Life
(500 – 1000 words, for writers aged 17 and under)

All the details, the rules and lots of tips on how to make a better story of life, can all be found on our website:
http://storiesoflife.net/

www.ingramcontent.com/pod-product-compliance
Lightning Source LLC
Chambersburg PA
CBHW052307300426
44110CB00035B/2167